Hermione and Her Little Group of Serious Thinkers

Don Marquis

Contents

- PROEM 7
- SINCERITY IN THE HOME 10
- VIBRATIONS 13
- AREN'T THE RUSSIANS WONDERFUL? 16
- HOW SUFFERING PURIFIES ONE! 18
- UNDERSTANDING, AND ONE'S OWN HOME 22
- THOUGHTS ON HEREDITY AND THINGS 25
- THE SWAMI BRANDRANATH 28
- FOTHERGIL FINCH, THE POET OF REVOLT 30
- HOW THE SWAMI HAPPENED 34
- TO HAVE SEVEN WIVES 34
- THE ROMANTIC OLD DAYS 37
- HERMIONE'S BOSWELL EXPLAINS 39
- SYMBOLS AND DEW-HOPPING 40
- THE SONG OF THE SNORE 43
- BALLADE OF UNDERSTANDING 49
- HERMIONE ON FASHIONS AND WAR 50
- URGES AND DOGS 54
- MOODS AND POPPIES 56
- CONCENTRATION 59
- SOUL MATES 62
- THE WORLD IS GETTING BETTER 68
- WAR AND ART 69
- A SPIRITUAL DIALOGUE 72
- WILL THE BEST PEOPLE RECEIVE THE SUPERMAN SOCIALLY? 74
- THE PARASITE WOMAN MUST GO! 77
- THE HOUSE BEAUTIFUL 80
- MAMA IS SO MID-VICTORIAN 82
- VOKE EASELEY AND HIS NEW ART 84
- HERMIONE ON SUPERFICIALITY 89
- ISIS, THE ASTROLOGIST 91
- THE SIMPLE HOME FESTIVALS 95
- CITRONELLA AND STEGOMYIA 98
- HERMIONE'S SALON OPENS 102
- THE PERFUME CONCERT 106
- ON BEING OTHER-WORLDLY 109
- PARENTS AND THEIR INFLUENCE 110
- FOTHERGIL FINCH TELLS OF HIS REVOLT AGAINST ORGANIZED SOCIETY 114
- THE EXOTIC AND THE UNEMPLOYED 117
- SOULS AND TOES 119
- KULTUR, AND THINGS 124
- THE SPIRIT OF CHRISTMAS 127
- POOR DEAR MAMA AND FOTHERGIL FINCH 130
- PRISON REFORM AND POISE 134
- AN EXAMPLE OF PSYCHIC POWER 135
- SOME BEAUTIFUL THOUGHTS 139
- THE BOURGEOIS ELEMENT AND BACKGROUND 142
- TAKING UP THE LIQUOR PROBLEM 144
- THE JAPANESE ARE WONDERFUL, ... 147
- IF YOU GET WHAT I MEAN 147
- SHE REFUSES TO GIVE UP THE COSMOS 150

THE CAVE MAN	152
THE LITTLE GROUP GIVES A PAGAN MASQUE	156
SYMPATHY	158
BLOUSES, BURGARS AND BUTTERMILK	162
TWILIGHT SLEEP	164
INTUITION	166
STIMULATING INFLUENCES	169
POLITICS	172
HERMIONE ON PSYCHICAL RESEARCH	174
ENVOY	177

HERMIONE AND HER LITTLE GROUP OF SERIOUS THINKERS

BY

Don Marquis

HERMIONE

PROEM

(Introducing some of Hermione's Friends)

I visited one night, of late,
Thoughts Underworld, the Brainstorm Slum,
The land of Futile Piffledom;
A salon weird where congregate
Freak, Nut and Bug and Psychic Bum.

There, there, they sit and cerebrate:
The fervid Pote who never potes,
Great Artists, Male or She, that Talk
But scorn the Pigment and the chalk,
And Cubist sculptors wild as Goats,
Theosophists and Swamis, too,
Musicians mad as Hatters be--
(E'en puzzled Hatters, two or three!)
Tame anarchists, a dreary crew,
Squib Socialists too damp to sosh,

Fake Hobohemians steeped in suds,
Glib females in Artistic Duds
With Captive Husbands cowed and gauche.

I saw some Soul Mates side by side
Who said their cute young Souls were pink;
I saw a Genius on the Brink
(Or so he said) of suicide.
I saw a Playwright who had tried
But couldn't make the Public think;
I saw a novelist who cried,
Reading his own Stuff, in his drink;
I saw a vapid egg-eyed Gink
Who said eight times: "Art is my bride!"

A queen in sandals slammed the Pans
And screamed a Chinese chant at us,
the while a Hippopotamus
Shook tables, book-shelves and divans
With vast Terpsichorean fuss . . .
Some Oriental kind of muss . . . .

A rat-faced Idiot Boy who slimes
White paper o'er with metric crimes--
He is a kind of Burbling Blear
Who warbles Sex Slush sad to hear
And mocks God in his stolen rhymes
and wears a ruby in one ear--
Murder to me: "My Golden Soul
Drinks Song from out a Crystal Bowl. . . .
Drinks Love and Song . . . my Golden Soul!"
I let him live. There were no bricks.

Or even now that Golden Soul
were treading water in the Styx.

A Pallid Skirt -- Anemic Wisp,
As bloodless as a stick of chalk --
Got busy with this line of talk:
"The Sinner is Misunderstood!
How can the Spirit enter in,
Be blended with, the Truly Good
Unless through Sympathy with Sin?"

"Phryne," I murmured, sad and low,
"I pass the Buck--I do not know!"

Upon a mantel sat a Bust. . . .
Some Hindu god, pug-faced and squat;
A visage to inspire disgust. . . .
Lord Bilk, the Deity of Rot. . . .
Nay, surely, 'twas the great god Bunk,
For when I wunk at it, it wunk!

I heard . . . I heard it proved that night
That Fire is Cold, and Black is White,
That Junk is Art, and Art is Junk,
That Virtue's wrong, and Vice is right,
That Death is Life, and Life is Death,
That Breath is Rocks, and Rocks are Breath:--

The Cheap and easy paradox
The Food springs, hoping that it shocks. . . .

Brain-sick I stumbled to the street
And drooled onto a kindly Cop:

"Since moons have feathers on their feet,
Why is your headgear perched on top?
And if you scorn the Commonplace,
Why wear a Nose upon your Face?
And since Pythagoras is mute
on Sex Hygiene and Cosmic Law,
Is your Blonde Beast as Bland a Brute,
As Blind a Brute, as Bernard Shaw?
No doubt, when drilling through the parks,
With Ibsen's Ghost and Old Doc Marx,
You've often seen two Golden Souls
Drink Suds and Sobs from Crystal Bowls?"

"I ain't," he says, "I ain't, Old Kid,
And I would pinch 'em if I did!"

"Thank God," I said, "for this, at least:
The world, in spots, is well policed!"

SINCERITY IN THE HOME

SINCERITY should be the keynote of a life, don't you think?

Sincerity -- beauty -- use -- these are my watchwords.

I heard such an interesting talk on sincerity the other evening. I belong to a Little Group of Serious

Thinkers who are taking up sincerity in all its
phases this week.

We discussed Sincerity in the Home.

So many people's homes, you know, do not
represent anything personal.

The SINCERE home should be full of purpose and
personality -- decorations, rugs, ornaments, hangings
and all, you know.

The home shows the soul.

So I'm doing over our house from top to bottom,
putting personality into it.

I've a room I call the Ancestor's Room.

You know, when one has ancestors, one's ancestral
traditions keep one up to the mark, somehow.
You know what I mean -- blood will tell, and all that.
Ancestors help one to be sincere.

So I've finished my Ancestors' Room with all
sorts of things to remind me of the dear dead-and-gone
people I get my traditions from.

Heirlooms and portraits and things, you know.

Of course, all our own family heirlooms were
destroyed in a fire years ago.

So I had to go to the antique shops for the portraits and furniture and chairs and snuff boxes and swords and fire irons and things.

I bought the loveliest old spinet -- truly, a fine!

I can sit down to it and image I am my own grandmother's grandmother, you know.

And it's wonderful to sit among those old heirlooms and feel the sense of my ancestors' personalities throbbing and pulsing all about me!

I feel, when I sit at the spinet, that my personality is truly represented by my surroundings at last.

I feel that I have at last achieved sincerity in the midst of my traditions.

And there's a picture of the loveliest old lady . . . old fashioned costume, you know, and all that . . . and the hair dressed in a very peculiar way. . . .

Mamma says its a MADE-UP picture -- not really an antique at all -- but I can just feel the personality vibrating from it.

I got it at a bargain, too.

I call her -- the picture, you know -- after an ancestress of mine who came to this country in the old Colonial days.

With William the Conqueror, you know -- or
maybe it was William Penn. But it couldn't have
been William Penn, could it? For she went to New
Jersey -- Orange, N.J. Was it William of Orange?
More than likely . . .

Anyhow, I call the picture after her -- Lady Clarissa,
I call it. She married a commoner, as so
many of the early settlers of this country did.

When I sit at the spinet and look at Lady Clarissa
I often wonder what people do without family
traditions.

And its such a comfort to know I'm in a room
that really represents my personality.

VIBRATIONS

Have you thought much about Vibrations?

We're taking them up this week -- a Little
Group of Advanced Thinkers I belong
to, you know -- and they're wonderfully worth
while -- WONDERFULLY so!

That's what I always ask myself -- is a thing
WORTH WHILE? Or isn't it?

Vibrations are the key to everything. Atoms

used to be, but Atoms have quite gone out.

The thing that makes the new dances so wonderfully beneficial, you know, is that they give you Vibrations.

To an untrained mind, of course, Vibrations would be dangerous.

But I always feel that the right sort of mind will get good out of everything, and the wrong sort will get harm.

The most interesting woman talked to us the other night -- to our little group, you know -- on one-piece bathing suits and the Greek spirit.

Don't you just done on the Greeks?

They have some of the most MODERN ideas -- it seems we get a lot of our advanced thought from them, if you get what I mean.

They were so UNRESTRICTED, too. One has only to look at their friezes and vases and things to realize that.

And the one-piece bathing suit, so the woman said, was an unconscious modern effort to get back to the Greek spirit.

She had a husband with her. He does lecture or anything, you know.

But she isn't so very Greek-looking herself, although her spirit is so Greek, so she has this Greek-looking husband to wear the sandals and the tunics and the togas and things.

She calls him Achilles.

It's quite proper, you know -- Achilles stays behind a screen until she wants to illustrate a point, and then he comes out with a lyre or a lute or something, and just stands there and LOOKS Greek. And then he goes back behind the screen and changes into the next garment she needs.

Of course, there are lots of men couldn't stand it as well as Achilles. But when you come to that, there are lots of men who don't look so very well in bathing suits, either.

And, of course, our American men don't have the temperament to carry off a thing like that.

Of course, if we all turned Greek it would be quite a shock at first to see everybody come into a dining-room or a drawing-room looking like Achilles does.

Not that temperament makes so much difference as it did a few years ago, you know -- temperament and personality are going out and individuality is coming in.

Have you thought much about automatic writing?

It's being taken up again, you know.

Not the vulgar, old-fashioned kind of
spiritualism -- that was so ordinary, wasn't it?

The new ghosts are different. More -- more --
well, more REFINED, somehow, you know. Like the
new dances as compared with that horrid turkey trot.

One should always ask one's self: "Does this
have a refining influence on me; and through me on
the world?"

For, after all, there is a duty one owes to society
in general.

Have you seen the new sunshades?

AREN'T THE RUSSIANS WONDERFUL?

Aren't the Russians marvelous people!

We're been taking up Diaghileff in a serious
way -- our little group, you know -- and
really, he's wonderful!

Who else but Diaghileff could give those lovely

Russians things the proper accent?

And accent -- if you know what I mean -- accent is everything!

Accent! Accent! What would art be without accent?

Accent is coming in -- if you get what I mean -- and what they call "punch" is going out. I always thought it was a frightfully vulgar sort of thing, anyhow -- punch!

The thing I love about the Russians is their Orientalism.

You know there's an old saying that if you find a Russian you catch a Tartar . . . or something like that.

I'm sure that is wrong. . . . I get so MIXED on quotations. But I always know where I can find them, if you know what I mean.

But the Russian verve isn't Oriental, is it?

Don't you just dote on verve?

That's what makes Bakst so fascinating, don't you think? -- his verve

Though they do say that the Russian operas don't analyze as well as the German or Italian ones -- if you get what I mean.

Though for that matter, who analyzes them?

One may not know how to analyze an operate, and
yet one may know what one likes!

I suppose there will be a frightful lot of imitations
of Russian music and ballet now. Don't you
just hate imitators?

One finds it everywhere -- imitation! It's the sincerest
flattery, they say. But that doesn't excuse it,
do you think?

There's a girl -- one of my friends, she says she
is -- who is trying to imitate me. My expressions,
you know, and the way I walk and talk,
and all that sort of thing.

She gets some of my superficial mannerisms . . .
but she can't quite do my things as if they were her
own, you know . . . there is where the accent
comes in again!

HOW SUFFERING PURIFIES ONE!

Oh, to go through fire and come out purified!
Suffering is wonderful, isn't it? Simply WONDERFUL!

Hermione and Her Little Group of Serious Thinkers

The loveliest man talked to us the other night --
to our Little Group of Serious Thinkers, you know
-- about social ideals and suffering.

The reason so many attempts to improve things
fail, you know, is because the people who try them
out haven't suffered personally.

He had the loveliest eyes, this man.

He made me thin. I said to myself, "After all,
have I suffered? Have I been purified by fire?"

And I decided that I had -- that is spiritually,
you know.

The suffering -- the spiritual suffering -- that I
undergo through being misunderstood is something FRIGHTFUL!

Mamma discourages every Cause I take up. So does Papa.

I get no sympathy in my devotion to my ideals.
Only opposition!

And from a child I have had such a high-strung,
sensitive nervous organization that opposition of
any sort has made me ill.

There are some temperaments like that.

Once when I was quite small and Mamma
threatened to spank me, I had convulsions.

And nothing but opposition, opposition, opposition now!

Only we advanced thinkers know what it is to suffer! To go through fire for our ideals!

And what is physical suffering by the side of spiritual suffering?

I so often think of that when I am engaged in sociological work. Only the other night -- it was raining and chilly, you know -- some of us went down in the auto to one of the missions and looked at the sufferers who were being cared for.

And the thought came to me all of a sudden: "Yes, physical suffering may be relieved -- but what is there to relieve spiritual suffering like mine?"

Though, of course, it improves one.

I think it is beginning to show in my eyes.

I looked at them for nearly two hours in the mirror last evening, trying to be quite certain.

And, you know, there's a kind of look in them that's never been there until recently. A kind of a -- a ----

Well, it's an INTANGIBLE look, if you get what I mean.

Not exactly the HUNGRY look, more of a YEARNING look!

Thank heaven, though, I can control it -- one should always be captain of one's soul, shouldn't one?

I hide it at times. Because one must hide one's suffering from the world, mustn't one?

But at other times I let it show.

And, really, with practice, I think I am going to manage it so that I can turn it off and on -- if you get what I mean -- almost at will.

Because, you know, in certain costumes that look will be QUITE unbecoming.

Quite out of Harmony. And Inner Beauty only comes through Inner Harmony, doesn't it?

Harmony! Harmony! Oh, to be in accord with the Infinite!

Nearly every night before I go to bed I ask myself, "have I vibrated in tune with the Infinite today, or have I failed?"

UNDERSTANDING, AND ONE'S OWN HOME

It's TERRIBLE when one can't get understanding in one's own family!

Papa has very little real sympathy for my advanced ideas. And as for Mamma!

Sometimes I think I shall WRITE!

Express myself, my real Ego, in Song.

Not rhymes, of course. If I worked a year I couldn't make two lines rhyme.

But rhyme is going out, anyhow.

Vers Libre is all the rage now.

We took it up not long ago -- our Little Group of Serious Thinkers, you know -- and I feel confident it is My Medium of Expression.

It is so untrammeled, isn't it?

And one should be untrammeled, both in Art and Life, shouldn't one?

Often I ask myself, at the close of day: "Have I been untrammeled today? Or have I FAILED?

If I could put my real Ego -- and how wonderful

the Ego is, isn't it? -- into vers libre, even Papa
might understand me.

I have always yearned to be understood!

I have drawn back from matrimony again and
again because I thought: "Will he understand me?
Will he see my real Ego? Or will he not?"

Only the other evening I was talking to the loveliest
man, who has been misunderstood by his wife.
It is FRIGHTFUL!

He is a sculptor. A cubist sculptor. But he
looks quite respectable -- really, some very good
people receive him.

And he has the most wonderful eyes -- sympathetic,
you know, and psychic -- but oh! so pure, too!

He dotes on purity. He told me that.

His wife does not understand him. She does
not see his real Ego.

He said to me: "I can read you like an open
book. You are yearning. You are yearning for
real understanding. No one has EVER understood you.
Is that not so? Is that not your secret?

Alas! It was. I could not deny it.

I said to him: "But is real understanding EVER attainable?"

He sighed and said: "Alas! The Unattainable!"

I knew why he sighed--there is so much of it -- the Unattainable!

"What one attains," I said, "is often so intangible -- do you not find it so?"

"Alas!" he said, "the Intangible!"

And I felt, somehow -- in a queer psychic way that is elusive, you know -- strengthened and sweetened spiritually by our sad little talk.

Our real Egos had been in communion. That's what he said.

He has nine very commonplace children, and his wife is very difficult socially.

She insists on filling some sort of commercial position, although he says her place is in the home.

So they have grown apart. People don't invite her places. Only him.

Oh! to be understood!

THOUGHTS ON HEREDITY AND THINGS

Isn't Heredity wonderful, though!

We've been going into it rather deeply --
My little Group of Serious, you know.

And, really, when you get into it, it's quite complicated.
All about Homozygotes and Heterozygotes, you know.

The Homozygotes are -- well, you might call
them the aristocrats, you know; thoroughbreds.

And the Heterozygotes are the hybrids.

Only, of course, they don't need to be goats at
all.

Not but what they COULD be goats, you know, just
as easily as horses or cows or human beings.

But whether goats or humans, don't you think
the great lesson of Heredity is that Blood will Tell?

Really the farther I go into Philosophy and
Science and such things the more clearly I see what a
fund of truth there is in the old simple proverbs!

People used to find out great truths by Instinct,
you know; and now they use Research -- vaccinate
guinea pigs, you know, and all that sort of thing.

Instinct! Isn't Instinct wonderful!

And Intuition, too!

You know, I have the most remarkable intuition at times! Have I ever told you that I'm frightfully psychic?

Mr. Finch, the poet -- you know Fothergil Finch, don't you? -- he writes vers libre and poetry both -- Mr. Finch said to me the other evening, "You are EXTREMELY psychic!"

"How did you know it?" I asked him.

"Ah!" he said, "how DOES one know these things?"

And how true that is, when you come to think it over! How DOES one know?

He has the great magnetic eyes! I could feel them drawing my thoughts from me as we talked.

"You have a secret," he said.

"Yes," I said. And to myself I added, "Alas!"

"Your secret is," he said, "that there is a difference between you and the other girls."

It was positively uncanny! I'VE felt that for years! But no one else had ever suspected it before.

"Mr. Finch," I said, "I must have TOLD you that --
or else it was just a wild guess. You COULDN'T have
gotten it psychically. HOW did you know it?"

"One knows these things," he said -- a trifle sadly,
I thought. "They come to one -- out of the

Silences; one knows not how. It is better not to
ask how! It is better not to question! It is better
to accept! Do you not feel it so?

Sometimes I think that Fothergil Finch is the
only man who has ever understood me.

You see, I am Dual in my personality.

There is the real Ego, and there is the Alter Ego.

And, besides these, I have so many moods which
do not come from either one of my Egos! They
come from my Subliminal Consciousness!

Isn't the Subliminal Consciousness wonderful;
simply WONDERFUL?

We're going to take it up in a serious way some
evening next week, and thresh it out thoroughly.

But I must run along. I have an engagement
with my dressmaker at two o'clock. You know,
I've really found one who can make my gowns
interpret my inner spirit.

THE SWAMI BRANDRANATH

I HEARD such a lovely lecture the other night
on the Cosmos.

A Little Group of Advanced Women that I
belong to are specializing this winter on the Cosmos.

We took it up, you know, because the other topics
we were studying included it so frequently. And
it's wonderful, really WONDERFUL!

Of course, an untrained mind will grapple with
it in vain. One's interest must be serious and sincere.
One must devote time to it.,

Otherwise one will get more harm than good
out of it, you know.

It's like the Russian dances that way.

They are so primal, those dances! And all those
primal things are dangerous, don't you think?
Unless one has poise!

It's odd, too, that some of the most primal
people have the most poise, isn't it?

The Swami Brandranath was like that. I've told
you bout the Swami Brandramath, haven't I?

He wore such lovely robes! You can't buy silk like that in this country.

And he had such a PURE look in this eyes. So many of these magnetic people lack that pure look, you know.

He used to give talks to a Little Group of Serious Thinkers I belong to.

He taught us to go into the Silences -- only we never quite learned, for some of the girls would giggle. There are always people like that. The dear Swami! -- he was so patient! It was Occidental levity, he said, and we couldn't help it.

That is one of the main differences between the Orient and the Occident, you know.

How wonderful they are, the Orientals. And just think of India, with all its yogis and bazaars and mahatmas and howdahs and rajahs and things!

He was a Brahmin, the Swami was. A Brahmin and a Burman are the same thing, you know.

It's a caste, like belonging to one of our best families.

The Swami explained about the marks of caste, and so forth, to us.

And then one of the girls asked him if he was tattooed!

The idea!

FOTHERGIL FINCH, THE POET OF REVOLT

Isn't it odd how some of the most radical and advanced and virile of the leaders in the New Art and the New Thought don't look it at all?

There's Fothergil Finch, for instance. Nobody could be more virile than Fothy is in his Soul. Fothy's Inner Ego, if you get what I mean, is a Giant in Revolt all the time.

And yet to look at Fothy you wouldn't think he was a Modern Cave Man. Not that he looks like a weakling, you know. Butwell, if you get what I mean -- you'd think Fothy might write about violets instead of thunderbolts.

Dear Papa is ENTIRELY mistaken about him.

Only yesterday dear papa said to me, "Hermione, if you don't keep that damned little vers libre run away from here I'll put him to work, and he'll die of it."

But you couldn't expect Papa to appreciate Fothy.

Papa is SO reactionary and conservative.

And Fothy's life is one long, grim, desperate
struggle against Conventionality, and Social
Injustice, and Smugness, and the Established Order, and
Complacence. He is forever being a martyr to the
New and True in Art and Life.

Last night he read me his latest poem -- one of his
greatest, he says -- in which he tries to tell just what
his Real Self is. It goes:

Look at me!
Behold, I am founding a New Movement!
Observe me. . . . I am in Revolt!
I revolt!
Now persecute me, persecute me, damn you,
   persecute me, curse you, persecute me!
Philistine,
Bourgeois,
Slave,
Serf,
Capitalist,
Respectabilities that you are,
Persecute me!
Bah!
You ask me, do you, what am I in revolt against?
Against you, fool, dolt, idiot, against you, against
   everything!
Against Heavy, Hell and punctuation . . . against
   Life, Death, rhyme and rhythm . . .
Persecute me, now, persecute me, curse you,
   persecute me!

Slave that you are . . . what do Marriage,
   Tooth-brushes, Nail-files, the Decalogue,
   Handkerchiefs, Newton's Law of Gravity, Capital,
   Barbers, Property, Publishers, Courts, Rhyming
   Dictionaries, Clothes, Dollars, mean to Me?

I am a Giant, I am a Titan, I am a Hercules of
   Liberty, I am Prometheus, I am the Jess Willard
   of the New Cerebral Pugilism, I am the Mod-
   ern Cave Man, I am the Comrade of the Cosmic
   Urge, I have kicked off the Boots of Superstition,
   and I run wild along the Milky Way
   without ingrowing toenails,
I am I!
Curse you, what are You?
You are only You!
Nothing more!
Ha!
Bah! . . . persecute me, now persecute me!

Fothy always gets excited and trembles and
chokes when he reads his own poetry, and while
he was reading it Papa came into the room and
disgraced himself by asking if there was
any MONEY in that kind of poetry, and Fothy
was so agitated that he fairly screamed when he
said:

"Money . . . money . . . curse money! Money
is one of the things I am in revolt against. . . .

Money is death and damnation to the free spirit!"

Papa said he was sorry to hear that; he said one
of his companies needed an ad writer, and he didn't
have any objection to hiring a free spirit with a
punch, but he couldn't consider getting anyone to
write ads that hated money, for there was a salary
attached to the job.

And Fothy said: "You are trying to bribe me!
Capitalism is casting its net over me! You are trying
to make me a serf: trying to silence a Free
Voice! But I will resist! I will not be enslaved!
I will not write ads. I will not have a job.

And then Papa said he was glad to hear Fothy's
sentiments. He had been afraid, he said, that Fothy
had matrimonial designs about me. And the
man who married HIS daughter would probably have
to stand for possessing a good deal of wealth, too,
for he had always intended doing something very
handsome for his son-in-law. So if Fothy didn't
want money, he wouldn't want me, for an enormous
amount of it would go to me.

Papa, you know, thinks he can be awfully sarcastic.

So many Earth Persons pride themselves on their
sarcasm, don't you think?

And Papa is an Earth Person entirely. I've got
his horoscope. He isn't AT ALL spiritual.

But you can image that the whole scene was
FRIGHTFULLY embarrassing to me -- I will NEVER forgive Papa!

And I haven't made up my mind AT ALL about
Fothy. But what I do know is this: once I get my
mind made up, I WILL NOT stand for opposition form
ANY source.

One must be an Individualist, or perish!

HOW THE SWAMI HAPPENED TO HAVE SEVEN WIVES

Isn't it terrible about that elephant at the Zoo
-- Oh, you know! -- it's like Gunga Din, only,
of course, it isn't Gunga Din at all.

Anyhow, he's CHAINED FOR LIFE! I suppose some-
one gave him tobacco for a joke and it made him
cross. I've heard of those cases, haven't you?

An elephant is such a -- such a -- well, NOBLE beast,
isn't he?

It's transmigration of souls makes them that way,
perhaps.

Oh is it a Rajah?

Anyhow, it sits on top of an elephant.

Hermione and Her Little Group of Serious Thinkers

We took up transmigration of souls one time --
our little Group of Serious Thinkers, you know --
and it's wonderful; simply WONDERFUL!

That was when the Swami Brandranath used to
talk to us. The dear Swami! Such eyes -- so pure
and yet so magnetic! -- I have never seen in a human
being.

The eye is the window of the soul, you know.

He's in jail now, the poor, dear Swami. But he
wasn't really a bigamist at all. You see, he had
seven spiritual planes. All of us do, only most of
us don't know it. But he could get from one plane
to another quite easily.

Of course, he couldn't remember what he'd done
on one plane while he was on the next one above
or below it. And that's the way he happened to
have seven wives -- one for each spiritual plane.

Only the Court took a sordid view of it. It seems
there was something about life insurance mixed
up with it, too.

The Occidentals are so apt to miss the spiritual
sweetness of the Oriental, don't you think?

We are -- all but the Leaders of Thought, and a
little group, here and there -- so commonplace.

Don't you LOATHE the commonplace?

Not loathe, really, of course -- because the harmonious
mind does not let itself be disturbed.

The harmonious mind realizes that dirt is only
useful matter in the wrong place, as Tennyson sings
so sweetly somewhere.

Tennyson has quite gone out, of course. He is
so -- so, well, if you get what I mean -- so mid-
Victorian, somehow.

It seems he WAS mid-Victorian all the time, but
it's only recently that it's been found out on him.

Though I always will think of "come Into the
Garden, Maud," as one of the world's sweetest
little epics.

I'm very independent that way, in spite of the
critics. After all, criticism comes down to a question
of individual taste, doesn't it? That is, in the
final analysis.

Independence! That is what this age needs.
Nearly every night before I got to bed I say to myself:
"Have I been independent today? Or have I FAILED?"

I believe in those little spiritual examinations,
don't you?

It helps one to keep in tune with the Infinite, you
know.

The Infinite! How much it comprises! And
how little we really understand it!

We're going to take it up, the Infinite, in a serious
way soon -- our Little Group of Advanced
Thinkers, you know.

THE ROMANTIC OLD DAYS

It must have been terribly difficult getting around
in the days before automobiles were invented,
or railroads or anything like that.

Though, of course, it was wonderfully romantic,
too.

The old coaching days, particularly, when everybody
blew on horns as they drove from town to
town, and there were highwaymen and cavaliers
with swords and all those people, you know, riding
by the coaches.

Don't you just DOTE on romance? I do!

But, of course, there's no place for it in our hurried
modern life, and I suppose we shouldn't regret it.

But now and then I sigh over it. Like dropping
a tear, you know, in a dear old chest perfumed with

lavender and old roses.

I always say that one can be advanced and in
the van of modern progress, and still drop a tear,
you know.

Do you think that all this study of sex hygiene
means the death of romance?

It's a serious thought, isn't it?

But what I always say is: "Which of these
things will do the most GOOD in the world?"

Especially good to the POOR!

You know how frightfully interested I am in the poor.

I make that my test. I always say to myself:
"Which will do the most good to the great masses?"

I take such a serious interest in the MASSES!

We should think twice before we take romance out
of their lives and replace it with science of any kind.

For, after all, you know, they represent the Future.

We should all think of the Future.

That's what makes the Feminist Movement such
a WONDERFUL thing -- it is moving right straight ahead
toward the Future!

I'm thinking of being a Suffragist again. I was once, you know, but I resigned.

The sashes and banners are such a frightful shade of yellow, you know. So I quit.

Beauty, after all, is the chief thing. What, after all, do all our reforms come to, if the world is not to be made more beautiful because of them?

And I simply CANNOT wear yellow.

HERMIONE'S BOSWELL EXPLAINS

Believe me, 'tis not with elation
  I dwell on Hermione's madness;
The result of my rapt contemplation
  Is sadness, a terrible sadness!

I weep when I note how she drivels;
  I sigh o'er her fake philanthropies;
I am pained when I see how she frivols,
  Like a kitten, with serious topics.

It is grief that her mental condition
  Inspires, not laughter or scorning;
If she has any use, 'til her Mission
  To stand as a Horrible Warning.

I am moral, essentially moral;
  I am grave, and hate everything trashy,
And that is the reason I quarrel
  With intellects flighty and flashy.

I yearn for the truth, I am earnest;
  I yearn to face facts without blinking,

Of all of my years, quite the yearnest
  Is my yearn to be thorough in thinking.

That's why I'm severe with this darling,
  Nor pardon nor whitewash nor gloss her, --
The linnet -- the parrot -- the starling!
  I weep over her and expose her.

SYMBOLS AND DEW-HOPPING

Last week the Loveliest man lectured to us --
to our Little Group of Serious Thinkers,
you know -- on the Ultimate Symbolism. In
art and life both, you know.

It was simply wonderful -- WONDERFUL!

Art, you know, used to be full of symbolism.

But now, it seems, symbolism has dropped out
of Art, and Nature has taken it up.

Odd, isn't it? But really not surprising when you come to think about it.

For, you know, Nature is always trying to keep up with advanced ideas -- evolving and evolving toward the Superman.

And the Superwoman, too.

I think it is the duty of us who are advanced thinkers to give Nature a worthy idea to evolve toward, don't you?

To set Nature a mark to come up to, you know.

For what is the use of evolution if it doesn't evolve forward instead of backward?

And the Best People, I think, should feel a sense of social responsibility and give evolution a model.

Each should be a Symbol -- that's what I always ask myself each night now: "Have I been a Symbol today? Or have I failed to be a symbol?"

Down at the beach last week I nearly drowned -- you don't mean to say you haven't heard of it? It was frightful.

I'd always heard that, when a person sinks, his whole past life passes before him in review.

But it didn't with me. What I said as I went

down was: "Have I been a Symbol? Or have I failed?"

And the life guard who got me out -- he was simply the most gorgeous man! -- burned bronze, you know, and with shoulders like a Greek god! -- and with the most wonderful eyes and white teeth -- he asked me, the guard did, "What, marm?"

It was fearfully disappointing! Sometimes they are college men, you know, just life-guarding through the summer. But would any college man have said, "What, marm?"

And then he went and saved a blonde creature in the most scandalous bathing suit I ever saw.

He saved one in the most business-like way, too, as if he were a waiter, you know, passing from one table to another.

No wonder the social fabric is crumbling when quite impossible people like life guards permit themselves to become blase' over such matters!

The lower classes are very discouraging anyhow, don't you think? -- after all we do for them in the way of philanthropy and sociology and uplifting them generally, you know!

Of course, I haven't lost my interest in sociology -- not by any means. I always hold fast the thought that all the world are brothers.

I'm taking up Dew-hopping next week. It's a
wonderful new nerve cure. Formerly it was quite
the thing to walk barefoot in the dew at dawn.

But at this new place I've discovered they don't
merely walk -- that's going out, quite. They HOP.
Like frogs and toads, you know.

It brings the patients into closer kinship with the
electric currents of the earth, hopping does, the
doctor says. It's WONDERFUL!

He is the loveliest man -- with mystic eyes! -- the
doctor is.

THE SONG OF THE SNORE

Fothergil Finch, Hermione's friend, the
vers libre poet, dodges through life harried
and hunted by one pursuing Fear.

"Some day," he said to me --

(It is Hermione's Boswell who is speaking in this
sketch, in the first person, and not Hermione, the
incomparable.) --

"Some day," Fothergil finch said to me, the
other night, in a tone of intense, bitter conviction,

"some day It will get me! Some day I will overtake
me. The great Beat, Popularity, which pursues me!
Some day It will clutch me and tear me
and devour my Soul! Some day I will be a
Popular Writer!"

It is my own impression that Fothergil's fears
are exaggerated; but they are very real to him. He
visualizes his own soul as a fugitive climbing higher
and higher, running faster and faster, to escape
this Beast. Perhaps Fothergil secretly hopes that
the speed of his gong will induce combustion, and
he will leap from the topmost hills of Art, flaming,
directly into the heavens, there to burn and shine
immortality, an authentic star. Well, well, we all
have our little plane, our little vanities!

"Fothergil," I said, cheerily, "Popularity has not
overtaken you yet. Cheer up -- perhaps it never
will."

We were in Fothergil's studio in Greenwich Village,
where I had gone to see how his poem on
Moonlight was getting along. He strode to the
window. Fothergil is not tall, and he is slightly
pigeon-toed -- the fleshly toes of Fothergil symbolize
the toes of his ever-fleecing soul -- but he strides.
Female poets undulate. Erotic male poets saunter.
Tramp poets lurch and swagger. Fothergil, being
a vers libre poet, a Prophet of the Virile, a Little
Brother of the Cosmic Urge, is compelled by what
his verse is to stride vigorously across rooms as if
they were vast desert places, in spite of what

his toes are. He strode magnificently, triumphantly,
to the window and flung the shade up and looked
out at the amorphous mist creeping
in across the roofs. The crawling fog must
have suggested his great, gray Dread, for presently
he turned away with a shudder and sank upon a
couch and moaned.

'Ah, Heaven! Popularity! The disgrace of it --
the horror of it! Popularity! Ignominy! When it
catches me -- when it happens ----"

He plucked from his pocket a small phial and held
it up toward the light and gazed upon it desperately
and raptly.

"I am never without this!" he said. "It is my
means of escape. I will not be taken unawares!
I carry it always. At night it is beneath my pillow.
The day it happens -- the moment I feel myself in
the grip of Popularity----"

I caught his hand; in his excitement he was
raising the poison to his lips.

"What I cannot understand, Fothergil," I said,
"is why a Poet of the Virile, a Reincarnation of the
Cave Man -- excuse me, but that is what you are
being this year, is it not ? -- should give way to Fear.
Is it not more in character to meet this Beast and
slay It? Is there not a certain contradiction between
your profession and your practice?"

"More than a contradiction," he said eagerly. "It is more than contradictory! It is paradoxical!"

I eliminate much that followed. When Fothergil gets started on the paradox, time passes. He is never really interested in things until he has discovered the paradoxical quality in them. Sometimes I think that his enthusiasm over himself is due to the fact that he discovered early in life that he himself was a paradox -- and sometimes I think that discovery is the explanation of his enthusiasm for the paradox.

"What," said Fothergil, "is the most paradoxical thing in the world? The Human Snore! It seems Ugly-yet it is Beautiful! It seems a trivial function of the body -- and yet it is the Key to the Soul ----"

"The Key to the Soul?"

"Man sleeps," he said, "and his Conscious Mind is in abeyance. But his Subconscious Mind is still awake. It functions. It has its opportunity to utter itself. The Snore is the Voice of the Soul! And not only the Soul of the individual but of the Soul of the race. All the experiences of man, in his ascent from the mire to his present altitude, are retained in the Subconscious Mind-his fights, his struggles, his falls, his recoveries. And his dreams and nightmares are racial memories of these things. Snores are the language in which he expresses them. Interpret the Snore, and you have the psychic history of the ascent of man from Caliban to Shakespeare!

"And I can interpret it! I have listened to a million Snores, and learned the language of the Soul! Night after night, for years, I harked to the Human Snore -- in summer, hastening from park bench to beach and back again; in winter, haunting the missions and lodging houses. Ah, Heavens! with what devotion, with what passion of the discoverer, have I not pursued the Human Snore! I have gone miles to listen to some snore that was reported to be peculiar; I have denied myself luxuries, pleasures, and at times even food, in order to hire reluctant persons to Snore for me!

"And I have written the Epic of the Snore in vers libre. You shall hear the prelude!"

And this is Fothergil's prelude:

Snore me a song of the soul,
Oh, sleeper, snore!
Whistle me, wheeze me, grunkle and grunt, gurgle
  and snort me a Virile stave!
Snore till the Cosmos shakes!
On the wings of a snore I fly backward a billion
  years, and grasp the mastodon and I tear him
  limb from limb,
And with his thigh hone I heat the dinosaur to
  death, for I am Virile!
Snore! Snore! Snore!
Snore, O struggling and troubled and squirming

    and suffering and choking and purple-faced
      sleeper, snore!
Snore me the sound of the brutal struggle when the
    big bull planets bellowed and fought with one
    another. in the bloody dawn of time for the
    love of little yellow-haired moons,
Snore!
Snore till Chaos raps with his boot on the walls of
    Cosmos and kicks to the landlord!

Turn, choke, twist and struggle, sleeper, and snore
     me the song of life in the making,
Sneeze me a universe full of star-dust,
Snore me back to the days when I was a Cave Man,
    and with my bare hands slew the walrus, for
    I am Virile!
Snore the death-rattle of the walrus, O struggling
    sleeper, snore!
Snore me ----

But I was compelled to leave. There is a great
deal of it, Fothergil says. If you know Fothergil
you are aware that when he declaims his Virile
verses he becomes excited; he swells physically;
sometimes he looks quite five feet tall in his moments
of expansion; all this is very bad for him.
More than once the declamation of his poem,
"Myself and the Cosmic Urge," has sent him shaking
to the tea urn.

Before I left I was able to calm him somewhat.
But with calm came reflection. And with reflection

came his great, gray Dread again.

When I left,. Fothergil was looking out of the
window and shuddering, as if the Monster
Popularity might be hiding behind the neighboring
chimneys. One hand clasped the phial caressingly.

But somehow I doubt that Fothergil will ever be
compelled to drink the poison.

BALLADE OF UNDERSTANDING

"Does not the World's stupidity
At times make Serious Thinkers fret?"
I asked the fair Hermione;
  "Sometimes," she said, "and yet . . . and
    yet .

We feel we owe the World a debt!"
She waved a slim, bejeweled hand,
She brooded on some vague regret. .
  "I hope," she sighed, "you'll UNDERSTAND!"

"Is not your high Philosophy
Too subtle for the Mob to get?"
I asked . . . She pondered seriously;
  "Sometimes," she said, "and yet . . . and
    yet . . .

She trifled with an amulet

Imported from some Orient land. . . .
"What fish can burst the Cosmic Net? . . .
  I HOPE," she sighed, "you'll Understand."

"Art, Science and Psychology,
Causes that rise and shine and set,

Do all these never weary thee?" --
  "Sometimes," she said, "and yet . . . and yet .
Would Thought and Life have ever met
Unless" . . . She paused. Her lashes fanned
Her eyes, with tears of ardor wet. . . .
  "I hope," she sighed, "YOU'LL Understand!"

"Princess, is Bull the One Best Bet?"-
  "Sometimes," she said, "and yet . . . and yet
She mused, and then; in accents bland,
"I hope," she said, "you'll UNDERSTAND!"

HERMIONE ON FASHIONS AND WAR

ISN'T war frightful, though; simply FRIGHTFUL!

What Sherman said it was, you know.

Though they say there's an economic
condition back of this war, too.

We took up economics not long ago -- our Little
Group of Serious Thinkers, you know -- and gave

an entire evening to it.

It's wonderful; simply WONDERFUL!

Without economics, you know, there couldn't be
any Civilization.

That's a thought that should give one pause,
isn't it?

Although, of course, this war may destroy
civilization entirely.

If I thought it was likely to do that I would join
in the Peace Demonstration at once -- or have they
had it already ? -- the march for peace, you know!
Anyhow, no matter what the personal sacrifice
might be, I would join in. Not that I care to march
in the dust. And black never did become me. But
I suppose there will be some autos. And, well --
one must sacrifice.

For if Civilization dies out, what will become of
us then?

Will we revert to the Primordial?

Will the Cave Man triumph?

The very idea gives me the creeps!

Because, you know, the Cave Man is all right --
and the Primitive, and all that -- as a protest against

Decadence-and in a LITERARY way -- but if ALL men were Cave Men!

Well, you know, the thought is frightful; simply frightful!

You can have a feeling for just ONE Cave Man,
you know, in the midst of Civilization, when a
MILLION Cave Men would ----

But the idea is too terrible for words!

And in this crisis it is Woman who must save the world.

The loveliest woman -- she's quite advanced,
really, and has the most charming toilettes -- told
our Little Group of Serious Thinkers the other
night that this is the time when Woman must rule
the world.

It is the test of the New Woman.

If ANYTHING is saved from the wreck it will be
because of Her.

She can write letters to the papers, you know,
against war and-and all that sort of thing, you know.

And, of course, if the Germans and Russians and
English do all get together and conquer Paris,
I suppose they won't kill the modistes and designers.

Civilization, you know, is not so easily killed
after all. The Romans were conquered, you know,
but all their styles and philosophies and things were

taken up by the Medes and Persians who conquered
them, and have remained unchanged in those
countries ever since.

But in a time like this, it's comforting to have
a Cause to cling to.

No matter what happens, the advanced thinkers
must cling together and make their Cause count.

And if England should conquer France, and put
a king on the throne there again, no doubt there will
be a great revival of fashion, as there was in the
days of Napoleon I. and the Empress Eugenie.

But if all the advanced thinkers in the world
could only get together in one place and THINK Peace
and Harmony -- sit down in circles, you know, and
send Psychic Vibrations across the ocean -- who can
tell but what the war might not end ?

The triumph of mind over matter, you know.

I'm going to propose the idea to our little group
and pass it on to all the other little groups.

I'd be willing to give up an entire evening to it myself.

URGES AND DOGS

We had quite a discussion the other evening
-- our Little Group of Serious Thinkers,
you know -- as to whether it was Idealism
or Materialism that had gotten the Germans into
this dreadful war.

Isn't Idealism just simply wonderful!

Fothy Finch said it was neither; he said it was
the Racial Urge.

It's like the Cosmic Urge, you know; except it's
altogether German, Fothy explained.

Every once in a while you hear of a New Urge.
That's one of the things that distinguishes Modern
Thought from the old philosophies, don't you
think?

Although, of course, the Cosmic Urge isn't what
it used to be a year or two ago.

It's become -- er -- well, VULGARIZED, if you know
what I mean. EVERYBODY'S writing and talking
about it now, don't you know.

I think, myself, it's going out soon. And a
leader -- a real pioneer in thought, you know,
would scarcely care to talk about it now without a

smile.

I've just about dropped it myself. It's the same way with everything exclusive. It soon becomes common.

Really, I hadn't worn my white summer furs three weeks before I saw so many imitations that I just simply HAD to lay them aside.

Don't you think people who take up things like that, after the real leaders have dropped them, are frightfully lacking in SUBTLETY?

Oh, Subtlety! Subtlety! WHAT would modern thought be without Subtlety?

Personally, I just simply HATE the Obvious. It's so -- so -- well, so easily seen through, if you know what I mean.

Fothy Finch said to me only the other day, "Has it ever occurred to you, Hermione, that you are NOT an Obvious sort of Person?"

It is almost UNCANNY the way Fothergil Finch can read my thoughts sometimes. We are both so very psychic.

Mamma said to me last night, "You are seeing a great deal of Mr. Finch, Hermione. Do you think it is right to encourage him if you don't intend to marry him? What ARE your intentions with regard to Mr. Finch?"

I didn't answer her at all -- poor dear Mamma is SO old-fashioned!

But I thought to myself ----

Well, would it be so IMPOSSIBLE?

Of course, marriage is a serious thing. One must look at it from all points of view, if one has a Social Conscience.

He has a LOVELY way with dogs, Fothy has. They trust him instinctively -- he is just DEAR with them. I have some beauties now, you know. They are getting so they won't let anyone but Fothy bathe them.

MOODS AND POPPIES

We took up the Bhagavad Gita -- our Little Group of Advanced Thinkers, you know -- in quite a thorough way the other evening.

Isn't the Bhagavad Gita just simply WONDERFUL!

It has nothing at all to do with Bagdad, you know -- though at first glance it seems quite like it might, doesn't it?

Hermione and Her Little Group of Serious Thinkers

Of course, they're both Oriental -- aren't you just
simply WILD about Oriental things? But really,
they're QUITE different.

The Bhagavad Gita, you know, is all about
Reincarnation and Karma, and all those lovely old
things.

When I start my Salon I'm going to have a
Bhagavad Gita Evening -- all in costume, you know.

I find that when I dress in harmony with the
Idea I RADIATE so much more effectively, if you
get what I mean.

Fothergil Finch is the same way.

He writes his best vers libre things in a purple
dressing-gown.

There's an amber-colored pane of glass in his
studio skylight, and he has to sit and wait and wait
and wait until the moonlight falls through that pane
onto his paper, and then it only stays long enough
so he can write a few lines, and he can't go on with
the poem until he comes again.

He brought me one last night -- he wrote it to me
  yes, really! -- and he waited and waited for
enough moonlight to do it, and caught a terrible
cold in his head, poor dear Fothy.

It goes like this:

Poppies, poppies, silver poppies in the moonlight,
  poppies!
Silver poppies,
Silver poppies in the moonlight,
Youth!
Poppies poppies, crimson poppies in the sunset,
  Love!
Poppies, poppies, poppies!
Black poppies in the midnight,
Death!
Three colors of poppies!
One color is silver,
The second color is crimson,
The third color is black,
And if there were a fourth color it would be
green!

Alas! Why is there never a fourth color?

Poppies, poppies, poppies, but no Green Poppy!

I asked the little crippled girl who sells poppies to
  Buy bread for the drunken father who beats her,

And she said, "I, too, seek the fourth color!"

I asked the boy who drives the grocer's delivery wagon, the old apple woman without teeth, the morgue keeper, the plumber, the janitor, the red-armed waffle baker in the window of a restaurant full of marble-topped tables and

pallid-looking girls, the subway guard and the
millionaire,

And they all said,
"Poppies, poppies, poppies,
We have never known but three colors!"
I am a Great Virile Spirit;
I, with my Ego,
I will give the world its Desire!
I, the strong!
I, the daring!
I will create a Green Poppy!

That about being Virile is just like Fothy! He
prides himself on being Virile, you know -- Poor
dear Fothy!

He said until he saw me he had always been satisfied
with silver and red and black poppies, but
as soon as he knew me he felt there MUST be a
Green Poppy somewhere.

It is likely a mood of my soul, you know -- the
Green Poppy is!

Isn't it simply wonderful!

CONCENTRATION

Isn't it just simply terrible the way the Balkans

are bombarding Venice . . . all those beautiful
Doges and things, you know.

I suppose there will be nothing left, just simply
nothing, of the city that Byron wrote about in
in -- what was it? Oh, yes, in "Childe Harold to
the Dark Tower Came."

That's one comforting thing to think of if this
country ever gets into a war, isn't it? I mean that
we haven't any of those lovely old things that can
be bombarded, you know.

I suppose if we ever did get into war someone
like Edison would invent something quick, you
know, and it would be all over in a few hours.

Isn't inventive science wonderful! Just simply
wonderful!

It's so -- so -- well, so DYNAMIC, if you get what I
mean. Isn't it?

Don't you just DOTE on dynamic things?

Dynamic personalities, especially.

I've often thought if I had it to do over again
I'd go in less for psychics and more for dynamics.

But then there are so many things that a modern
thinker must keep up with, aren't there?

And it's easy enough to concentrate one's mind on
one or two things, but I often find it terribly difficult
to concentrate on ten or twelve different things
all at the same time.

And one must if one is to keep up with the very
latest in Thought and Life.

Concentration! Concentration! That is the key
to it all! Nearly every night when I am alone with
my own Ego I go into the Silences for a little period
of Spiritual Self-Examination and I always ask
myself: "Have I Concentrated today? Really
Concentrated? Or have I failed?"

I call these little times my Psychic Inquisitions.

In the hurry of this crowded age one must find
time to get along with one's self, must one not?
Fothy Finch has written a beautiful thing about the
hurry of this crowded age which I wish everyone
could hang over his desk.

Well, I must be going on now. I have a committee
meeting for this afternoon. I can't for the
life of me remember whether it's about suffrage --
Oh, yes, I marched! -- or about some relief fund.

SOUL MATES

I'm taking up Bergson this week.

Next week I'm going to take up Etruscan
vases and the Montessori system.

Oh, no, I haven't lost my interest in sociology.

Only the other night we went down in the auto
and watch the bread line.

Of course, one can take up TOO MANY things.

It's the spirit in which you take up a thing that
counts.

Sometimes I think the spirit in which you take
a thing up counts more than the thing itself -- counts
in its effect on you, you know.

Of course, the way to get the real meaning out
of any thing is to put yourself in a receptive attitude.

In serious things the attitude counts for everything.
One mustn't scoff.

If you look seriously and scientifically you'll'
see there's a great deal more than you suspected
in all this affinity and soul mate craze, for instance.

Not that I care much for the words "soul mate"

and "affinity" particularly; they have been so VULGARIZED, somehow.

The Best People don't use those terms any more.

Psychic harmony is the new term.

The loveliest man explained all about it to us the other day. I belong to a Little Group of Thinkers, who take a serious interest in these things, you know.

We are trying to find out how to make our psychic powers count for the betterment of the world. I am very psychic. Some are now.

This man had the most interesting eyes and the silkiest beard, and he said his aura was pink.

If he should meet a girl, you know, with an aura just the shade of pink that his aura is, why then they would know they were in psychic harmony.

Simple, isn't it? But then all truly great ideas ARE simple, aren't they?

But if his aura was blue, and her aura was yellow, then, of course, they would quarrel. That's what makes so much domestic unhappiness.

But he said something that gave me the most frightfully insecure feeling.

He said the aura CHANGES its color as the soul progresses.

Two people may be in harmony today, and both have pink auras, and in a year hers may be green and his golden.

What desperate chances a woman takes when she marries, doesn't she?

I sometimes think life must have been a much more comfortable thing before the world got to be so terribly advanced.

But, of course, it is our duty to sacrifice personal comfort for the future of the race and the betterment of the world.

As I was looking at the bread line the thought came to me that the chief difference between this advanced age and other ages was in the fact that people today are willing to take a serious interest in such things.

People are willing to sacrifice themselves today, you know.

It is food for optimism, don't you think?

Not that I was really so uncomfortable in the auto, you know. I had on my new mink coat.

HERMIONE TAKES UP LITERATURE

We've been going in for Astrological
Research lately -- our Little Group of
Modern Thinkers, you know -- and we've
picked our own personal stars.

Only it seems such a shame, doesn't it, that one
isn't allowed to CHANGE stars? Keeping the same
star all your life is rather monotonous, don't you
think?

Though, of course, if one changed and got some-
one else's star things might be frightfully
complicated, mightn't they?

But it would make a charming little story,
wouldn't it, for a girl to change stars, you know,
and find that her new star belonged to some quite
nice young man, and, of course, after that, their
destinies would be one.

I get some of the most ORIGINAL plots for stories!

Fothergil Finch has often said to me that that
is one difference between genius and talent. When
you have genius, you know, things like that just
come to you; but if you only have talent you must
work and WORK for them.

"If I only hd your spontaneity, Hermione!"
Fothergil often says.

And really, it's never been any trouble for me at
all to dash off an idea, though of course they
would have to be touched up by the editors a little
before they could be printed.

Fothergil said the other night I should try poetry.

"Why, Fothy," I said, "if I lived a hundred years
I never could make two lines rhyme with each
other!"

But he said Rhyme was out of fashion anyhow,
and -- would you believe it? -- while we were talking
I got an idea for a poem and just dashed it off
then and there -- a vers libre poem you know, and it
goes:

> What becomes of
> People when they die?
> I used to ask when I was a little child,
> And now even since
> I am grown up I am not sure that I know!

"Fothy," I said, "It was so easy -- that makes me
afraid it isn't really good!"

"Ah," he said, "that modesty PROVES you are a
genius! Heavens, what would I not give to
have you spontaneity, your modesty, your spontaneity --"

But I interrupted him. Another idea had come
to me -- just like that, and -- would you believe it?

I dashed off another one, right then and there! It went:

> I see the rain fall.
> It is no effort for the rain to fall.
> Why is it no effort?
> Because it falls spontaneously!
> O Spontaneity! Spontaneity!
> Rain is genius,
> Genius is rain!
> Fall, fall, rain!

Fothy is going to get them printed -- he knows a lot of vers libre publishers -- if Papa will only put up the money. And one nice thing about poor dear Papa is that he always will put it up.

So that night I wrote twenty or thirty more of them, and they were ALL good -- ALL works of genius -- they ALL came to me just like the first ones!

The last one came to me just as I was going to bed. I looked out of the window and saw the moon and ran and got a pencil and wrote:

> I see the moon out of the window.
> I wonder what it thinks of me?
> Wouldn't the moon and I both be surprised
> If we found that neither of us
> Though anything at all about the other?

The book's going to be vellum, you know, and that sort of thing. I'm going to have a gown just like the cover and give a fete when it comes out.

The worst thing about being literary, though, is
that it makes one feel so RESPONSIBLE for the gift,
if you know what I mean, doesn't it?

THE WORLD IS GETTING BETTER

DR. JAGADES CHUNDER BOSE says that
plants are almost as sensitive as human beings --
they have feelings and susceptibilities,
you know, and all that sort of thing.

Isn't it wonderful how the Hindus find these
things out?

Soul speaking to soul, I suppose.

But I have scarcely been able to eat comfortably
since I read it.

Every time I sit down to a salad it makes me
feel quite like a cannibal!

And to think, I was just on the point of becoming
a vegetarian, too!

I suppose to be on the safe side one should eat
nothing but minerals.

But, of course, advanced thinkers will have to
take the matter up seriously and discover a way
out -- some day we will live on aromas and
electricity, no doubt.

Don't you think the world is getting kinder?
A hundred years ago, for instance, no one would
have cared whether plants suffer pain or not -- people
wouldn't have given it a second though, you know.

And now, though, they will have to keep on
eating them until something else is invented, they
will do it with a shudder and won't enjoy them near
so much. The world is losing much of its cruelty
and thoughtlessness. Upward! Onward! Is the
slogan.

Do you like my new coat? Unborn lamb skin,
you know. Isn't it lovely?

WAR AND ART

THIS war is going to have a tremendous in-
fluence on Art -- vitalize it, you know, and
make it REAL, and all that sort of thing.
In fact, it's doing it already. We took up the war
last night -- our Little Group of Serious Thinkers,
you know -- in quite a serious way and considered
it thoroughly in all its aspects and we decided
that it would put more SOUL into Art.

And into life, too, you know.

Already you can see it on every hand how much serious purpose it is putting into lives that were merely trivial before. Even poor, dear Mamma -- and really, it would be hard to imagine a more trivial person than Mamma! -- is knitting socks.

She is going to send them to the Poles. She wanted to send them to the Belgians.

But I said to her, "Positively, Mamma, you are ALWAYS behind the times. Don't you know the Belgians are going out and the Poles are coming in?"

And, you know, it's been months since really Smart People have knit for the Belgians. The Poles are QUITE the thing now.

It's strange how great movements keep going on and on from mountain peak to mountain peak of usefulness like that, isn't it? -- changing their direction now and then as evolution itself does, but always progressing, progressing!

That is one wonderful thing about evolution -- it ALWAYS progresses.

When one thinks it over, one grows more and more conscious that the human race owes a great deal to Evolution, doesn't one?

WHAT could we have done without it?

It's as somebody said about something else one time -- if we hadn't had it, you know, it would have been necessary to invent it, though for the life of me, I can't remember who it was or what he said about it. Although likely it was Madame de Stael. We took her up once and it developed that she had said a most surprising number of things like that things, you know, that would be quite quotable if you could only remember them.

Isn't memory a wonderful facility, though?

I've always intended to go in for developing mine systematically and scientifically.

But I've never done it because I always forget whether I should order the book-shop people to send home a work on numismatics or a work on mnemonics. One of them is about money, you know, and the other is about memory. And once when I was shopping and thought I had it right it turned out -- the book did, when I got it home -- to be all about air and things. Pneumatics, you know! Wasn't it perfectly ridiculous?

But, of course, one learns by one's mistakes.

Have you seen dear Nijinsky?

We were discussing him last evening -- our little group, you know -- and decided that while he has

more Personality than Mordkin he has less
Temperament, if you get what I mean.

One of the girls said last evening, "Mordkin is
more exotic, but Nijinsky is more esoteric."

And another said, "One of them shows intellect
obviously mingled with spirit, but the other shows
spirit occultly mingled with intellect."

Fothergil Finch said, "They are alike in their
differences, but subtly differentiated in their
likenesses, n'est-cd pas?"

Fothy has a simply delightful faculty of summing
a thing up in a sentence like that, but it makes him
very vain if you show you think so; so I put him
in his place and closed the discussion with one remark:

"It is all," I said, "it is ALL a question of Interpretation."

And, quite seriously, when you come to think
about it, it usually is, isn't it?

A SPIRITUAL DIALOGUE

Last night I met Hermione,
And eagerly she said to me:
"Thoughts from the ambient everywhere
Electrify our worldly air."

Hermione and Her Little Group of Serious Thinkers

"My soul," I said, "grabs off such hints
As butter, whether pats or prints,
Receives and holds all unaware
Small strands of drifting, golden hair.
But have YOU thought, O Maiden fair,
O, have you thought profoundly of
The psychic consciousness in crows?
Or why the Malay when in love
Wears rubber earrings on his toes?"

The lady shook her lovely head --
'Twas coiffed divinely -- and she said:
"Have you reflected on the part
Primeval instinct plays in Art?
It's simply wonderful the way
Old things grow new from day to day!"

"That's true," I said, "I often ape
The Ape to get my Art in shape --
And with the Simian going strong,
 Behold, another Rennysawng!"

"Perhaps," she said, "across the verge
Of darkness, from the Cosmic Urge,
The Light is speeding in bright waves,
E'en now to show the way to slaves!"

"The thought," I said, "is cheerful -- but
These Swamis WILL chew betel-nut!"

"Alas!" she said, "alas! too true!
But oh! it's wonderful of you

To sympathize and understand   --"
(She gestured with a jeweled hand) --
"The joy of being understood!"

"Our talk," I said, "has done me good."

WILL THE BEST PEOPLE RECEIVE THE SUPERMAN SOCIALLY?

WE'VE been taking up Metabolism lately -- our Little Group of Serious Thinkers, you know -- and it's wonderful; just simply WONDERFUL!

I really don't know how I got along for so many years without it -- it opens up such new vistas, doesn't it?

I can never think in the same way again about even the most trivial things since I have learned all about Protoplasm and -- and -- well, all these marvelous scientific things, you know.

Isn't Science DELIGHTFUL!

There's the Cosmos, for instance. It had always been there, you know. But nobody knew much about it until Scientists took it up in a serious way.

And now I, for one, feel that I couldn't do
without it!

Although, of course, one feels one's responsibilities
toward it too, and that is apt to be rather
trying at times unless one has a truly earnest nature
and is prepared to make sacrifices.

If the Cosmos is to be improved, what is there
that can improve it except Evolution?

And unless we who are serious thinkers give
Evolution a mark to reach, how can we be sure that
Evolution will Evolve in the right direction?

I have worried myself half to death at times
over the Superman!

You know I feel personally responsible, to a
certain extent, about what he will be like when he
gets here. If he isn't what he should be, you know,
it will be the fault of those of us who are the
leaders in thought today -- it will be because we
haven't started him right, you know.
Mamma -- poor dear Mamma is SO unadvanced,
you know! -- has an idea that when the Superman
does get here he won't be at all the sort of person
that one would care to receive socially.

"Hermione," she said to me only the other day,
"no Superman shall EVER come into MY house!"

She heard some of my friends, you know, talking

about the Superman and Eugenics, and she has
an idea that he will be horribly improper.

"I consider that the Superman would be a DANGEROUS
influence in the life of a young woman," said Mamma.

"Mamma," I told her, you are FRIGHTFULLY behind
the times! There isn't a doubt in the world that
when the Superman does come he will be taken
up by the Best People. Anarchists and Socialists
go everywhere now, and dress just like other people,
and ;you can hardly tell them, and it will be
the same way with the Superman."

What Mamma lacks is contact. Contact with --
with -- well, she lacks Contact, if you get what I
mean.

So many of the elder generation DO lack Contact,
don't you think?

Although, of course, it would be very hard to
have Contact and Background at the same time.

And if one must choose between Contact and
Background, the choice is apt to be puzzling at
times.

Although, of course, it is useless to reason too
much on things like that. Intuition often succeeds
where reason fails, especially if one is at all Psychic.

Well, I must go. I must hurry to my costumer's.

I'm have a special costume made, you know.
We've been taking up Spiritualism again -- our little
group, you know. And I'm going to give a Spirit
Fete, and of course it will take a great deal of
dressing and arranging and decoration.

Papa says it will be a Ghost Dance, but he is so
terribly frivolous and irreverent at times.

Don't you just simply LOATHE frivolity?

THE PARASITE WOMAN MUST GO!

THE Parasite Woman must go!

Our Little Group of Serious Thinkers
took up the Parasite Woman last night in
quite a thorough way. One of the most interesting
women you ever listened to gave us a little talk
about the Parasite Woman, you know.

And we decided that the Parasite Woman has
NOTHING to Contribute to the Next Generation.

Oh, these Parasite Women! It just simply makes
my blood boil to her about them! I don't know
when I have been so indignant!

With the world so full of work to be done for
the Cause -- for ALL the Causes, you know -- they
just sit around selfishly at home all wrapped up
in their own families, or children, if they're married,
and do nothing at all for the Evolution of
the Ego and the Development of the Race, and the
Conscious Guidance of the Next Generation, or
anything like that.

Thank goodness I could never be a Parasite Woman!

And, yet, I PITY them, too.

I'm thinking quite seriously of starting a little
Mission of my own for the purpose of appealing
to and reforming the Parasite Women among my
acquaintances.

Of course it will take organization, and that
means I will have money to start it and
keep it going.

But Papa will give me the money all right. That
is one thing about poor, dear Papa -- he doesn't
understand the new movements at all, but he WILL
give me money. And he never asks what I do
with it.

Now and then, of course, he scolds me a little -- he
told me the other day that I cost him nearly as much
as a war. But I can always jolly him, you know,
when he gets that way. Men are so easily managed
and flattered.

I suppose my Mission will take quite a LOT of money, too. But it is my DUTY, and I am willing to make ANY sacrifice -- we modern thinkers are used to making sacrifices for our Cause!

And it is worth a lot of sacrifice to make the Parasite Woman over into an Awakened and Enlightened Member of Society, independent of the Man-Made System that has shackled her for so long.

What is nobler than Emancipation?

Of course, I'll have to have a Secretary, And to get one especially training in organizing the Mission will cost quite a bit, probably.

But Papa will never miss it.

And I think I'll have a MAN for a Secretary. One that is quite presentable socially, you know. For the Secretary will have to attend to a lot of the details. I will give some teas and entertainments and things, just to get the Parasite Women I know interested.

And there's nothing like the right sort of a man to get women to cooperate in some Cause that aims for Woman's Liberty.

And I suppose, really, TWO Secretaries would be better. And they will have to be men who can dance the new dances well, too. That counts a lot nowadays in getting girls to come to places.

I feel that I have Found my Work! One's work lies at one's hand, if one could but see it, always. And mine is to Save the Parasite Women I know from Themselves and their Frivolity.

I will coax the first cheque out of Papa this very evening! It may take some management and jollying, but--well, Papa is EASY!

THE HOUSE BEAUTIFUL

WE'RE taking up the House Beautiful -- our Little Group of Serious Thinkers, you know -- for we've decided that Environment has more effect on personality than Heredity.

Interior decoration is the greatest of the arts -- don't you think? -- because it furnishes the proper setting for the spirit.

The loveliest woman gave us a talk on interior decoration the other night -- she wears these slinky, Greek things, you know, with straw sandals, when the weather permits -- and I engaged her to do the house over.

But right away a problem presented itself -- whether to have the house done to fit my personality or whether to have the house done to fit the thing

I want my personality to evolve into, and trust the environment to help in the evolution.

Modern thought complicates LIFE immensely, doesn't it?

But I always feel that it is my duty to give the best in myself to these problems.

Someone must help Evolution evolve. Someone must be unselfish enough to give the cosmos new marks to come up to.

And who but the serious thinkers are willing to sacrifice themselves?

Well, we finally decided to do every room in the house differently -- each one to fit a mood, you know.

There's one room now I call "Aspiration," where I go for my little spiritual examinations.

And the next room beyond that is "Resolve."

And then there's a room I call "Brotherly Love," where I go to think out how to help the masses.

For of course I haven't lost my interest in sociological problems.

In fact I'm having some new dresses made -- simple, quiet looking things, you know -- for the express purpose of visiting the very poor in and asking them questions about themselves.

Though I must admit that since helping the war sufferers came into fashion friendly visiting has rather gone out.

MAMA IS SO MID-VICTORIAN

WE'VE been taking ;up Hedonism lately --
our Little Group of Modern Thinkers,
you know -- and it's wonderful, just
simply WONDERFUL!

Though Mamma -- poor dear Mamma is so hopelessly old fashioned; -- has entirely the wrong idea about it.

"Hermione," she said to me the other evening, after the little talk, "WHAT did the lecturer call himself?"

"He's a Hedonist," I said.

"Indeed!" she said, "and what sort of modern impropriety is Hedonism? Is it something about Sex, or is it something about Psychics?"

I simply couldn't speak.

I just gave her a look and walked out of the room. It is absolutely useless to attempt to explain anything to Mamma.

She is so Mid-Victorian!

And Mid-Victorianism has quite gone out, you know. Really. The loveliest man gave us a talk on the Mid-Victorian recently, and when he was done there wasn't a one of us that didn't go and hide our Tennysons and Ruskins.

Although I always WILL like "Come into the Garden, Maud."

But he did it with such HUMOR, you know. Isn't a sense of humor a perfectly WONDERFUL thing?

A sense of humor is a sense of proportion, you know -- he brought that out so cleverly, the anti-Mid-Victorian man did.

Though so many people who have a sense of humor are so -- so, well so QUEER about it, if you get what I mean. That is, if you know they have one, of course you're naturally watching for them to say humorous things; and they're forever saying the sort of things that puzzle you, because you have never heard those things before in just that way, and if you DO laugh they're so apt to act as if you were laughing in the WRONG place!

And one doesn't dare NOT to laugh, does one? It's really quite unfair and unkind sometimes!

Don't you think so?

We took up a volume on The Analysis of Humor one winter -- our Little Group of Serious Thinkers, you know -- and read it completely through, and before the winter was over it got so there wasn't a one of us that dared NOT to laugh at anything any other one said and -- well, it got rather ghastly before spring. Because even if someone wanted to know if a person needed an umbrella someone else would laugh.

Well, I must be going now. I have a committee meeting at three this afternoon. We're going in for this one-day Women's Strike, you know -- our little group is.

VOKE EASELEY AND HIS NEW ART

FOR my acquaintance with Voke Easeley -- --

(Hermione's reporter, and not Hermione herself, is speaking now.) -- --

For my acquaintance with Voke Easeley and his new art, I am indebted to Fothergil Finch.

Fothergil is a kind of genius hound. He scurries sleuthing around the town ever on the scent of something queer and caviar. He is well trained and

never kills what he catches himself; he takes it to
Hermione; and after Hermione has tired of it I
am at liberty to do what I please with it.

The most remarkable thing about Voke Easeley
at a casual glance is his Adam's apple. It is not
only the largest Adam's apple I have ever seen, and
the hardest looking one, and the most active one,
but it is also the most intelligent looking one. Voke
Easeley's face expresses very little. His eyes are
small and full and green. His mouth, while large,
misses significance. His nose, indeed, is big; but
it is mild; it is a tame nose; one feels no more
character in it than in a false nose. His chin
and forehead retreat ingloriously from the battle
of life.

But all the personality which his eyes should
show, all the force which should dwell in his
nose, all the temperamental qualities that should
reveal themselves in his mouth and chin, all the
genius which should illumine his brow -- these dwell
within his Adam's apple. The man has run entirely
to that feature; his moods, his emotions, his
thoughts, his passions, his appetites, his beliefs, his
doubts, his hopes, his fears, his resolves, his
despairs, his defeats, his exaltations -- all, all make
themselves known subtly in the eccentric motions
of that unusual Adam's apple.

When I saw him first in action I did not at once
get it. He stood stiffly erect in the center of
Hermione's drawing-room, surrounded by the serious

thinkers, with his head thrown back and his Adam's apple thrust forward, and gave vent to a series of strange noises. Beside him stood a very slender lady, all dressed in apple green, with a long green wand in her hand, and on the end of the wand was an artificial apple blossom. This she waved jerkily in front of Voke Easeley's eyes, and his Adam's apple moved as the wand moved, and from his mouth came the wild sounds in response to it.

Soon I realized that she was conducting him as if he were an orchestra.

But still I did not get it. For it was not words, it was nothing so articulate as speech, that Voke Easeley uttered. Nor was it, to my ear, song. And yet, as I listened, I began to see that a wild rhythm pervaded the utterance; the Adam;'s apple leapt, danced, swung round, twinkled, bounded, slid and leapt again in time with a certain rough barbaric measure; the sounds themselves were all discords, but discords with a purpose; discords that took each other by the hand and kicked and stamped their brutal way together toward some objective point.

I led Fothergil into a corner.

"What is it?" I whispered. It is always well, at one of Hermione's soul fights, to get your cue before the conversation officially starts. If you don't know what is going to be talked about before the talk starts the chances are that you never will know from the talk itself.

"A New Art!" said Fothergil. And then he led me into the hall and explained.

What Gertrude Stein has done for prose, what the wilder vers libre bards are doing for poetry, what cubists and futurists are doing for painting and sculpture, that Voke Easeley is doing for vocal music.

"He is painting sound portraits with his larynx now," said Fothergil. "And the beautiful part of it is that he is absolutely tone deaf! He doesn't know a thing about music. He tried for years to learn and couldn't. The only way he knows when you strike a chord on the piano is because he doesn't like chords near as well as he does discords. He has gone right back to the dog, the wolf, the cave man, the tiger, the bear, the wind, the rock slide, the thunder and the earthquake for his language. He interprets life in the terms of natural sounds, which are discords nearly always; but he has added brains to them and made them all the moods of the human soul!"

"And the lady in green?"

"That is his wife -- he can do nothing without her. There is the most complete psychic accord between them. It is beautiful! Beautiful!"

When we returned the lady in green was announcing:

"The next selection is a Voke Easeley impression of the Soul of Wagner gazing at the sunrise from the peak of the Jungfrau."

The wand waved; the Adam's Apple leapt, and they were off. What followed cannot be indicated typographically. But if a cat were a sawmill, and a dog were a gigantic cart full of tin cans bouncing through a stone-paved street, and that dog and that cat hated each other and were telling each other so, it would sound much like it.

It was well received. Except by Ravenswood Wimble. He always has to have his little critical fling.

"The peak of the Jungfrau!" he grumbled. "Jungfrau indeed! It was Mont Blanc! It was very wonderfully and subtly Mont Blanc! But the Jungfrau -- never!"

"Hermione," I said, "what do you think of the New Art?"

"It's wonderful!" she breathed, "just simply wonderful! So esoteric, and yet so simple! But there is one thing I am going to speak to Mrs. Voke Easely about -- one improvement I am going to suggest. His ears, you know -- don't you think they are too large? Or too red, at least, for their size? They catch the eye too much -- they take away from the effect. Before he sings here again I will have Mrs. Easeley bob them off a little."

HERMIONE ON SUPERFICIALITY

AREN'T you just crazy about the Moral Uplift?

It's coming into every department of life now and one just simply HAS to keep up with it in order to talk intelligently these days.

Not that one can talk too freely about it in mixed company, you know.

There are getting to be the awfullest lot of moral subjects that one can't talk about generally, aren't there?

Eugenics and sex hygiene and all these plays and books with a moral purpose, you know.

Of course lots of people DO talk about them generally. I did myself for quite a while. And then another girl and I got some books and studied up what the things we had been talking of really were and it shocked us horribly!

Mamma has been trying to get me to give up the moral uplift entirely, but you've just simply GOT to talk it or be out of date.

Of course the whole thing depends upon whether

you are a serious thinker -- if you're sincere, REALLY
sincere, you can take up anything and get good out of it.

The loveliest man talked to us last night -- to our
Little Group of Advanced Thinkers, you know.

He said the curse of the age and the country was
superficiality. People aren't thorough, you know.

I've noticed that myself and I agree with him.
If one is going to take things up and show a serious
interest in them one must not limit one's self to a
few phases.

One must be broad. One must be thorough.
One must cover the whole field of thought.

Our little group this winter has been trying to
do that. So far we've take up Bergson, socialism,
psychology, Rabindranath Tagore, the meaning of
welfare work, culinary science, the new movements
in art -- and ever so many more things I can't re-
member now.

For the rest of Lent we're going to take up the
Cosmic Consciousness.

One of the girls thought it would be a nice sort
of thing to take up during Lent -- a quiet kind of
thing, you know; not like feminism or chemistry.

Have you seen any of the new parti-colored boots
yet?

Isn't it an absurd idea?

And yet, you know -- if it made for Beauty!

That is what one must always say to one's self must one not? I mean: Does it make for Beauty?

That's the reason I left the Suffrage Party, you know. They wanted me to wear one of those horrid yellow sashes. And my complexion can't stand yellow. So I quit the Suffrage Party right there.

ISIS, THE ASTROLOGIST

WE'RE taking up astrology quiet seriously -- our Little Group of Serious Thinkers, you know -- and we've hired the loveliest lady astrologer to cast our horoscopes and give us a talk and get us started right.

She wrote a letter to me--the most perfectly fascinating letter -- and I told her to call, and we looked her over. She wore a beautiful sky-blue gown with gold stars on it -- one of those Greek ones, you know, like poor, dear Isadora Duncan wore -- and a gold star in the middle of her forehead.

It makes her look like a unicorn, that star,"

Ravenswood Wimble said. But then nobody ever pleases Ravenswood Wimble completely. He is so -- if you get me.

"If a unicorn, then a celestial unicorn," Fothy Finch said. Fothy is too dear for anything; he is always hunting for the good in people, like Apollo, or Euripides -- which was it? -- when they gave him the basket full of wheat and chaff, and he separated them. Or maybe it was Diogenes.

She has six sisters, and they are all astrologers, and they call them the Pleiades.

Although Voke Easeley, in his horrid slangy way, said: "Pleiades? She's a Bear!"

Don't you just utterly loathe slang?

Bit I was going to tell you about the lovely letter she wrote -- that's what attracted me to her at the first.

"Have you never asked yourself," it began "'Why was I born?'"

Fancy knowing that about one! If there is one question I have asked myself thousands and thousands of times it is, "Why was I born?"

And then the letter went on to talk about horoscopes and the Inevitable.

"We may not overcome the inevitable," it said, "but it is ours to see that the Inevitable does not overcome us."

Oh, the Inevitable! The Inevitable!

How often I have thought of the Inevitable with despair!

And it has never occurred to me before that one could take it and use it as one pleased. But it seems one can if one knows about it beforehand. It is like Destiny that way. If one is ignorant of one's Destiny, it comes upon one with a surprise. But if one knows beforehand what one's Destiny is to be, one can make onself the master of it. That is where the horoscope comes in handy, you know.

After dipping into Astrology I will never again be afraid of the Inevitable.

As the Letter says: "Every woman with her horoscope before her, and her Soul back of her, should be able to solve any problem and meet any situation that may occur in her life."

Ravenswood Wimble wanted to know, when he met the lady -- did I tell you that her professional name is Isis? -- what would happen if her Soul was before her and her horoscope back of her. But Isis just simply froze him with a look.

Don't you think that levity is horrid in the midst

of vital affairs like that?

But I suppose every little group has someone in it that thinks he or she has to be quippy and facetious at times.

Not but what I have a sense of humor myself.

I think a sense of humor is the saving grace, if you get what I mean.

But no one should try to use it unless he is perfectly sure that everyone understands he is being humorous.

We are going to take up the sense of humor -- our Little Group of Thinkers, you know -- in a serious way soon.

But the Swami doesn't like Isis. Poor, dear Swami! She is a charlatan, he says. And she doesn't like him. "My dear," she said to me, "are you SURE he really goes into the Silences? Or does he just PRETEND to?"

Isn't it awful about geniuses that way -- how jealous they ARE of each other? Especially psychics! We had two mediums the same evening a year or two ago who actually quarreled over which one of them a certain spirit control belonged to.

THE SIMPLE HOME FESTIVALS

DON'T you just love the simple old festivals, like Thanksgiving Day and Christmas?

That's is one thing that Papa and Mamma and I agree about. And this year we had a very simple sort of Thanksgiving Day.

Of course, it's rather a bore if you have to invite a lot of relations.

But one must always sacrifice something to gain the worth-while things, mustn't one?

And what is more worth while than simplicity?

Simplicity! Simplicity! Isn't it truly WONDERFUL!

Nearly every night before I go to bed I ask myself: "have I been simple and genuine today? Or have I FAILED?

Papa always has two maiden aunts to Thanksgiving dinner. Dear old souls, I suppose, but frumps, you know.

And Fothergil Finch was there, too. I asked poor dear Fothy, because otherwise he would have had to eat in some restaurant.

I tried to be agreeable to Papa's aunts -- of

course. I suppose they are my great-aunts, but I never felt REALLY related to them -- but how could he know how terribly unadvanced they are?

Fothy's only real interests center about Art, you know. And if he had talked of Art it would have been better.

But, as he told me later, he thought he should try to meet my people on their own ground and talk of something practical.

Something with a direct bearing on life, you know.

So he asked Aunt Evelyn what she thought of Trial Marriages.

She didn't know exactly what he meant at first, but Aunt Fanny whispered something to her and she turned white and said, "Mercy!"

Poor dear Fothy saw he must be on the wrong track, so he changed the subject and began to tell Aunt Fanny the plot of a new problem play. One of the sex ones, you know.

"Heavens," said Aunt Fanny, and began to tremble.

And they drew their chairs nearer together and each one took a bottle of smelling salts out of a little black bag, and they sat and trembled and smelled their salts and stared at him perfectly fascinated.

This embarrassed Fothy, but he though his mistake
had been in talking about anything artistic,
like a play, so he changed the subject again. He
told me afterward that he felt if he could get onto
a really PRACTICAL subject all would go well.

So he asked Aunt Evelyn what she thought about Genetics.

"What are they?" asked Aunt Evelyn, her teeth chattering.

"Why, Eugenics," said Fothy. And then he had
to explain all about Eugenics.

They sat perfectly still and stared at him, and he
felt sure he had them interested at last, and he
talked on and on about Eugenics and the Future
Race, you know, and that led him back to Trial
Marriages, and then he go onto the Twilight Sleep.

And, as he said himself afterward, what could
be more practical?

But, you know, commonplace people never
appreciate the efforts that serious thinkers make for
them, and Aunt Evelyn refused to come to the
table at all when dinner was announced. She said
she had lost her appetite and felt faint.

But Aunt Emmy came. She asked the blessing.
Papa always has her do that on Thanksgiving Day
and Christmas and New Year's. And she made a
regular prayer out of it -- prayed for Fothy, you

know, right before him; and prayed for me too. It was awful.

And afterward poor dear Fothy said he wished he had talked about Art.

"It's safe," I said; "then people can't get offended, for nobody knows what you mean at all."

"Oh," said Fothy, "nobody does?" And he went away quite melancholy and injured.

CITRONELLA AND STEGOMYIA

WE were talking about famous love affairs the other evening, and Fothergil Finch said he was thinking of writing a ballad about Citronella and Stegomyia.

And, of course, everybody pretended they knew who Citronella and Stegomyia were. Mrs. Voke Easeley -- You've heard about Voke Easeley and his New Art, Haven't you? -- Mrs. Voke Easeley said:

"But don't you think those old Italian love affairs have been done to death?"

"Italian?" said Fothy, raising his eyebrows at Mrs. Voke Easeley.

You know, really, there wasn't a one of them knew who Citronella and Stegomyia were; but they were all pretending, and they saw Mrs. Voke Easeley was in bad. And she saw it, too, and tried to save herself.

"Of course," she said, "Citronella and Stegomyia weren't Italian lovers THEMSELVES. But so many of the old Italian poets have written about them that I always think of them as glowing stars in that wonderful, wonderful galaxy of Italian romance!"

Fothy can be very mean when he wants to. So he said:

"I don't read Italian, Mrs. Easeley. I have been forced to get all my information about Citronella and Stegomyia from English writers. Maybe you would be good enough to tell me what Italian poet it is who has turned out the most recent version of Citronella and Stegomyia?"

Mrs. Voke Easeley answered without a moment's hesitation: "Why, D'Annunzio, of course."

That made everybody waver again. And Aurelia Dart said -- she's that girl with the beautiful arms, you know, who plays the harp and always has a man or two to carry it about wherever she goes -- somebody else's husband, if she can manage it -- Aurelia said:

"D'Annunzio, of course! Passages of it have been set to music."

"Won't you play some of it?" asked Fothy, very politely.

"It has never been arranged for the harp," said Aurelia. "But if Mrs. Easely can remember some of the lines, and will be good enough to repeat them, I will improvise for it."

That put it up to Mrs. Easeley again, you know. She hates Aurelia, and Aurelia knows it. Voke Easeley carried Aurelia's harp around almost all last winter. And the only way Mrs. Easeley could break Voke of it was to bring their little girl along the one that has convulsions so easily, you know. And then when Voke was getting Aurelia's harp ready for her the little girl would have a convulsion, and Mrs. Easeley would turn her over to Voke, and Voke would have to take the little girl home, and Mrs. Easeley would stay and say what a family man and what a devoted husband Voke was, for an artist.

Well, Mrs. Easeley wasn't stumped at all. She got up and repeated something. I took up Italian poetry one winter, and we made a special study of D'Annunzio; but I didn't remember what Mrs. Easeley recited. But Aurelia harped to it. Improvising is one of the best things she does.

And everybody said how lovely it was and how much soul there was in it, and, "Poor Stegomyia! Poor Citronella!"

The Swami said it reminded him of some passages
in Tagore that hadn't been translated into
English yet.

Voke Easeley said: "The plaint of Citronella is
full of a passion of dream that only the Italian
poets have found the language for."

Fothy winked at me and I made an excuse and
slipped into the library and looked them up -- and,
well, would you believe it! -- they weren't lovers at
all! And I might have known it from the first, for
I always use citronella for mosquitoes in the country.

They were still pretending when I got back, all
of them, and Aurelia was saying: "Citronella differs
psychologically from Juliet -- she is more like
poor, dear Francesca in her feeling of the cosmic
inevitability of tragedy. But stegomyia had a strain
of Hamlet in him."

"Yes, a strain of Hamlet," said Voke Easeley.
"A strain of Hamlet in his nature, Aurelia -- and
more than a strain of Tristram!"

"It is a thing that Maeterlinck should have written,
in his earlier manner," said Mrs. Voke Easeley.

"The story has its Irish counterpart, too," said
Leila Brown, who rather specializes, you know, on
all those lovely Lady Gregory things. "I have always
wondered why Yeats or Synge hasn't used it."

"The essential story is older than Ireland," said the Swami. "It is older than Buddha. There are three versions of it in Sanskrit, and the young men sing it to this day in Benares."

Affectation! Affectation! Oh, how I abhor affectation!

It was perfectly HORRID of Fothy just the same.

ANYONE might have been fooled.

I might have been myself, if I were not too intellectually honest, and Fothy hadn't tipped me the wink.

HERMIONE'S SALON OPENS

I

Perchance last night you felt the world careen,
Leap in its orbit like a punished pup
Which hath a hornet on his burning bean?
Last night, last night -- historic yestere'en! --
Hermione's Salon was opened up!

II

Without, the night was cold. But Thought, within,

Roared through the rooms as red and hot as Sin.
Without, the night was calm; within, the surge
And snap of Thought kept up a crackling din
As if in sport the well-known Cosmic Urge
with Psychic Slapsticks whacked the dome and Shin
Of Swami, Serious Thinker, Ghost and Goat.
From soup to nuts, from Nut to Super Freak,
From clams to coffee, all the Clans were there.
The groggy Soul Mate groping for its Twin,
The burgling free verse Blear, the Hobo Pote,

Clairvoyant, Cubist bug and Burlapped Greek,
Souse Socialists and queens with bright green hair,
Ginks leading barbered Art Dogs trimmed and Sleek,
The Greenwich Stable Dwellers, Mule and Mare,
Pal Anarchs, tamed and wrapped in evening duds,
Philosophers who go wherever suds
Flow free, musicians hunting after eats,
And sandaled dames who hang from either ear
Strange lumps -- "art jools" -- the size of pickled beets,
Writers that write not, hunting Atmosphere,
Painters and sculptors that ne'er paint nor sculp,
Reformers taking notes on Brainstorm Slum,
Cave Men in Windsor Ties, all gauche and glum,
With strong iron jaws that crush their food to Pulp,
And bright Boy Cynics playing paradox,
And th' inevitable She that knitteth Belgian socks --
A score of little groups ! -- all bees that hum
About the futile blooms of Piffledom.

III

A wan Erotic Rotter told me that

The World could not be Saved except through Sin;
A she eugenist, sexless, flabby, fat,
With burst veins winding through unhealthy skin,
With loose, uncertain lips preached Purity;
A Preacher blasphemed just to show he dared;
A dame praised Unconventionality
In words her secretary had prepared;
A bare-legg'd painter garbed in Leopard hide
Quarreled with a Chinese lyre and scared the dogs;
A slithering Dancer slunk from side to side
In weird, ungodly, Oriental togs;
A pale, anemic, frail Divinity
Confided that she thought the great Blond Beast
Himself was Art's own true Affinity;
An Anarch gloomed; "The Mummy at the Feast
Gets all the pleasure from the festive board!"
I know not what they meant; I only wunk
Within myself, and praised the great god Bunk.
A Yogi sought the Silences and snored.

IV

But 'twas Hermione that Got the Hand!
Ah, yes, she talked! Of Purpose, and of Soul,
And how Life's parts are equal to its Whole.
And Thought -- and do the Masses Understand?
She lightly touched on Life and Love and Death,
And Cosmic Consciousness, and on Unrest,
Substance and Shadow, Solid Things and Breath,
The New Art movements her sweet voice caressed,
Philanthropy, Genetics, Social Duty,
The Mother-Teacher claimed a passing smile,
And she made clear we all must worship Beauty

And Concentrate on Things that are Worth While.
"Each night," she said, "each night ere I retire
Into the Depths I peer, and I inquire,
"Have I today some Worth-while Summit scaled?
Or have I failed to climb? Oh, have I failed?
These little talks between the Self and Soul --
Oh, don't you think? -- still help us toward the Goal;
They help us shape the Universal Laws
In sweet accordance with our glorious Cause!"
"Hermione," said I, "they do! They do!"
"Thank you," said she, "I KNEW you'd understand!"
I said to her, the while I pressed her hand,
"All, all, my interest I owe to you!"

And then I left, and following my feet
Soon found that they had led me to the street.

V

And there I found a burly Garbage Man
Who through bleak winter nights from can to can
Goes on his ashy way, sans rest or pause,
Goes on his way, still faithful to his Cause.

"Tell me," said I, "if now across the verge
Of night should come the kindly Cosmic Urge,
Strong-armed and virile, full of vim and help,
And offer you with thee here cans to help,
Would you accept the Cosmic Urge's aid,
Or would you rise up free and unafraid
And say, 'My restless Personality
Bids me return a negative to thee!'"

"Old scout," says he, "I've never really brought
My intellects to bear on that there though!
I gets no help, I asks no help from none --
But I have noticed, bo, that one by one,
And soon or late, and gradual, day by day,
Most things in life eventual comes my way!
Into the Ashes Can the whole world goes,
Old hats, old papers, toys and styles and clo'es,
Eventual they dump "em down the bay!"

VI

Symbolic Garbage Man! Sans rest or pause,
In steadfast faith work for thy Sacred Cause!
Some time, perhaps, all piles of twisted bunk,
All half-baked faddists, heaps of mental junk,
Unto the waiting Scow we'll cart away
Eventual to dump 'em down the bay!

THE PERFUME CONCERT

THE Loveliest man gave us a talk the other evening -- our Little Group of Serious Thinkers, you know -- on the Art of the Future.

And what do you think it is to be? You'd never guess! Never!

The entertainment of the future will be a

Perfume concert!

Every scent, if you get what I mean, corresponds to some color, and ever color corresponds to some sound, and every sound corresponds to some emotion.

And the truly esthetic person -- the one who is Sensitized, if you get what I mean -- will hear a tone on the violin, and see a color, and think passionately of the One he Loves, all at the same time, just through smelling a Rose.

Only, of course, it must be the RIGHT KIND of a rose.

Papa -- poor der Papa is so coarse and crude sometimes in his attempts to be witty -- Papa says it would be a fine idea to lead the man who talked to us into a boiled cabbage foundry and then watch him die of the noise. Papa is not Sensitized; he doesn't understand that the esthete really WOULD die -- Papa resists the vibrations of the esthetic environment with which I have striven to surround him, if you get what I mean.

Oh, to be Sensitized! To be Sensitized! To vibrate like a reed in the wind! To thrill like a petal in the sun!

I'm having a study of my aura made. You know, one's soul gives off certain colors, and if one's individuality is to be in tune with the Cosmic All, one must take care that the colors about out do not jar with one's own Psychic Hue.

And after one has found one's soul color, one can
find the scent to match that color, if you get what I
mean.

I am going to have the house re-decorated, with
a sweet subtle blending of perfumes in every room!

I have always been good at matching things,
anyhow -- I perceive affinities at a glance. Psychic
people do.

When I was quite a small child Mamma always
used to take me with her to the shops if there were
ribbons or anything like that to be matched.

I just loved it, even as a baby! And I think
it is the greatest fun yet.

Often I go through half a dozen shops, not because
I want to buy anything, but just to match colors,
you know. It gives me a thrill that nothing else does.

Some of us are like that -- some of us truly Sensitized
Souls -- we function, I mean, quite without
being able to stop it -- I hope you follow me. Isn't
it wonderful to be in touch with the Universe in
that way! Not, of course, that the shop girls who
show you the fabrics and things are always understanding.

The working classes are so often ungrateful to
us advanced thinkers. Sometimes I am almost provoked

to the point of giving up my Social Betterment work
when I think HOW ungrateful they are.
But some of us, in every age, must suffer at the
hands of the masses for the sake of the masses, if
you know what I mean.

ON BEING OTHER-WORLDLY

IT is not enough to be merely unworldly.

One must be OTHER-WORLDLY as well, if you
get what I mean.

For what does all Modern Thought amount
to if it does not minister to the Beautiful and the
Spiritual?

Isn't Materialism simply FRIGHTFUL?

For the undisciplined mind, I mean. Of course,
the right sort of mind will get good even out of
Materialism, and the wrong sort will get harm out
of it.

Every time before I take up anything new I ask
myself, "Is it OTHER-worldly? Or is it not OTHER-Worldly?"

We were going to take up Malthusianism and
Mendelism -- our Little Group of Serious Thinkers,
you know -- and give a whole evening to them, but

one of the girls said, "Oh let's NOT take them up.
They sound frightfully chemical, somehow!"

I said, "The question, my dear, is not whether
they are chemical or un-chemical. The question is,
Are they worldly? Or are they OTHER-Worldly?"

That is the Touchstone. One can apply it to
everything, simply EVERYTHING!"

Should teachers be mothers, for instance -- that
question came up for discussion the other evening.
And I settled the whole matter at once, with one
question: "Is it worldly? Or is it OTHER-worldly
for Teachers to be Mothers? Or is it merely Un-Worldly?"

Have you seen the latest models? Some of them
are wonderful, simply WONDERFUL! You know I
always dress to my temperament -- and I'm having
the loveliest gown made -- the skirt is ecru lace, you
know; a double tiered effect, falling from a straight
bodice, and the color scheme is silver and blue.

PARENTS AND THEIR INFLUENCE

MAMA is unadvanced enough, goodness
knows.

But poor, dear Papa!

Hermione and Her Little Group of Serious Thinkers

"Papa," I said to him the other day, " all conservatives worth listening to were radicals in their youth." The loveliest man told us that the other night -- our Little Group of Serious Thinkers, you know -- and it struck me as being profound.

And isn't profundity fascinating?

But Papa only glowered and said, "Umph!"

Papa, you know, is an obstructionist.

"Papa," I said to him, "what is stubbornness in you has become will power in me. You will never dominate me -- NEVER! You should study heredity; it's wonderful, simply WONDERFUL!

Papa scowled and said, "Umph!"

But you know, Parents are Doomed.

Our little group listened to a talk the other evening about Parents. Mothers, particularly.

"The menace of the Mother," it was called. I always make note of titles.

This man said -- he was a regular savant -- I wish you could have heard him -- my, if I weren't such an advanced thinker, I would be a savant ----

Anyhow, he said, this savant, that Mothers held back Civilization through Selfishness -- they teach

the Child, you know, that is -- er, well, you know,
they lose sight of Ulterior Ethics and Race Morality
while inculcating Individual Self-Improvement.

It's frightful to think about, isn't it? Simply FRIGHTFUL!

Then and there I resolved that if I were ever a Mother
I would turn over the up-bringing of my children to experts
and savants and specialists like that.

"Papa," I said, "you allowed poor, dear Mamma
to make me selfish -- you know you did! What
have you to say for yourself? What right had you
to make me a Self-Indulgent Individualist?

And, you know, I have struggled and struggled
to get rid of the selfishness my parents trained into
me. How I strive for Harmony and Humility!
Nearly every night before I go to bed I say to my-
self: "Have I been HUMBLE today? Truly humble?
Or have I FAILED?"

Children are not nearly SIMPLE enough these days.

Oh, for more Simplicity! That is what we all need.

Though I will say this for Mamma -- that it
would have been hard to train Simplicity into me
even if she had known how.

I had such a high-strung, sensitive, nervous organism
as a child, you know.

At a very early age my temperament began to show.

And one CANNOT hide one's temperament.

Especially if one is at all psychic, and I am, VERY.

But if I ever have Children -- well, I will take no chances with them.

To begin with, I will Select their Father.

Mamma said, when I told her that: "Hermione, you are HORRID!"

Poor dear Mamma! She's SO stupid! "Mamma," I said to her, of course I DON'T mean free love. I'm not that advanced, I hope! Though some VERY Nice People have written of it -- it's quite respectable, as a theory. But you're hopelessly old-fashioned. I WILL select the parent of my Off-spring; YOU were selected."

Mamma only groaned and said: "Anything but a Cave-man, Hermione."

But I am not sure. It comes back to me again and again how Primitive I am in some ways.

And to wander barefoot in the dew!

Not really quite barefoot, of course -- but with some of the new sandals on.

FOTHERGIL FINCH TELLS OF HIS REVOLT AGAINST ORGANIZED SOCIETY

BERTIE GRIGGS -- you know Ethelbert Griggs, don't you? He does the text for the Paris fashions for a woman's magazine, and on the side he writes the most impassioned verse. All about Serpents and Woman, and Lillith and Phryne, you know.

Bertie said to me only the other day, "Fothy, you are too Radical. It will keep you down in the world."

"Bertie," I said, "I know I am, but can I help it? I spurn the world! A truly virile poet must."

"Some day, Fothy," he said, "you will come into contact with the law."

I only laughed. Bitterly, I suppose, for Bertie looked at me quite shocked.

"Bertie," I said, "I expect persecution. I welcome it. All great souls do. I look for it. On one pretext or another, I will be flung into prison when my next volume, 'Clamor, Cries and Curses' comes out."

And I will, too, if I ever find a publisher who dares to bring it out. But they are all too cowardly!

"Fothy," he said, "you Revolutionists are always talking -- but what do you ever do?

I arose with dignity. "Bertie," I said, "I am ready to suffer for the Cause." I turned and left him. I must have been pale with resolve, for he ran after me and caught me by the wrist. But I shook him off.

I was in a desperate mood.

"Curses upon all their Conventions!" I said, as I turned up the street toward Central Park. "Curses upon all organized society!"

I stopped in front of Columbus's statue, at Columbus Circle.

"Fool," I muttered bitterly, "to discover a new world"

I shook my fist at the statue and went on.

I wandered over to the place where they keep the animals, and stopped in front of one of the monkey cages.

Dear, unconventional little beasts! They always charm my blacker moods away from me! So free, so untrammeled, so primitive!

I smiled at a monkey. He smiled at me. I held up a peanut. He reached out his hand for it.

I was about to fling it to him when I saw a sign that read:

"Visitors are warned not to feed the animals under the penalty of the law."

Always their laws! Always their restrictions! Always their damnable shackles! Always this denial of the rights of the individual!

For a moment I stood there with the peanut in my hand just simply too angry for anything!

And then I cried out, quite loudly: "Curses upon organized society! I will break its laws! I will feed the animals!"

Always in times of great crisis I see myself quite plainly as if I were some other person; poets often do, you know; and I could not help thinking of the pose of Ajax defying the lightning.

"I WILL break the law!" I cried. "So there!"

And with that I flung the peanut right into the cage with all my might, and ran away, laughing mockingly as I ran.

I felt that I had crossed the Rubicon, and that

night I sat down and wrote my revolutionary poem, "The Defiance."

What the Cause needs is men with Vision to see and Courage to perform! This is the age of Virility!

THE EXOTIC AND THE UNEMPLOYED

WE'VE been taking up the Exotic this week in poetry and painting, you know, and all that sort of thing -- and its influence on our civilization.

Really, it's wonderful -- simply WONDERFUL! Quite different from the Erotic, you know, and from the Esoteric, too -- though they'll all mixed up with it sometimes.

Odd, isn't it, how all these new movements seem to be connected with one another?

One of the chief differences between the Exotic in art and other things -- such as the Esoteric, for instance -- is that nearly everything Exotic seems to have crept into our art from abroad.

Don't you think some of those foreign ideas are apt to be -- well, dangerous? That is, to the untrained mind?

You can carry them too far, you know -- and if
you do they work into your subconsciousness.

One of the girls -- she belongs to the same Little
Group of Advanced Thinkers that I do -- has been so
taken with the Exotic that she wears orchids all the
time and just simply CRAVES Chinese food. "My
love," she said to me only yesterday, "I feel that I
must have chop suey or I'll DIE! The Exotic has
worked into her subliminal being, you know.

She has an intense and passionate nature, and
I'm sure I don't know what would become of her
if it were not for the spiritual discipline she gets
out of modern thought.

Next week we're taking up Syndicalism -- it's
frightfully interesting, they say, and awfully
advanced.

I suppose it's a new kind of philosophy or socialism,
or maybe anarchy -- or something like that.
[Most of these new things that come along nowadays
ARE something like that, aren't they.

I'm sure the world owes a debt to its advanced
thinking which it can never repay for always
keeping abreast of topics like that.

Not that I've lost my interest in any of the older
forms of sociology, you know, just because I am
keeping up with the newer phases of it.

Only yesterday I rode about town in the car and
had the chauffeur stop a while every place where
they were shoveling snow.

The nicest man was with me -- he is connected
with a settlement, and has given his life to sociology
and all that sort of thing.

"Just think," I said to him, "how much real practical
sociology we have right here before us -- all
these men shoveling snow -- and how little they realize,
most of them, that their work is taking them
into sociology at all."

He didn't say anything, but he seemed impressed.

And I'm not sure the unemployed should be grateful
to the serious thinkers for the careful study we
give them. Don't you think so?

SOULS AND TOES

I went to a Soul Fight at Hermione's

And nothing normal can describe it . . .

It was beyond rhyme, reason, rum, rhubarb or rhythm . . .

Therefore, Vers Libre Muse, help me!

Imagist outcast with the bleary eyes,

My psychic Pup, my polyrhythmic hound, lift up
  Your voice and help me howl!

Tenth Muse, doggerel muse, slink hither, brute,

And lick your master's hand . . . I've need of
  Thee . . .

Come catercornered on three legs with doubtful tail
  And eager eyes . . .

Tomorrow I may bash you in the ribald ribs again

And publicly disown you;

But oh! Today I've need of thee . . .

Winged mongrel, mutt divine, come here and help
  Me bay the piebald moon!

It was a Soul Fight at Hermione's . . .

A fat Terpsichore with polished toes . . . a barefoot she Soul

With ten Achaian toes . . . and each toe had a separate soul, she said . . .

Was there . . . not only there, but IT.

She sat upon a couch and lectured . . . not with words,

Hermione and Her Little Group of Serious Thinkers

But with her toes, her eloquent, her temperamental toes . . .

Her topes that had trod (so she said) the paths of beauty

Since Hector was a pup at Troy . . .

She sat upon a couch . . . bards, swamis and Hermione,

Gilt souls and purple, melomaniacs, yellow souls
  And blue,

Souse socialists and other cognac-scented cognoscenti,

Post-cubist chicles that would ne'er jell into gum . . .

All, all the little groups from all the brainstorm Slums . . .

Why specify? . . . we know our little groups!
  . . . where there . . .

Were there to worship at those feet . . . to vibrate
  and change color with the moods of those unusual feet. . . .

"This toe," she said, "is Beauty . . . this is Art . . .

This toe is Italy, and this is Greece." . . .

A poet, quite beside himself with inspiration,

Suddenly arose and cried:
  "This little pig went to market,
    This little pig stayed home

This little pig was Greece,
   This little pig was Rome!"

But they chilled him . . . he went Into the Silences . . .

And Terpischore resumed:

"My ten toes are: Beauty, Art, Italy, Greece,
   Life, Music, Psyche, Color, Motion, Liberty!
Put yourself into a receptive attitude now, and
   Beauty will speak to you!"
And while a satellite ran rosy fingers down a lute,
   she moved the toe named Beauty to and fro . . .

A hush fell on the assembled nuts, as Beauty moved . . .
As Beauty spoke to them . . .
"I see," murmured Hermione to Fothergil Finch,
   "I see,
As that toe moves . . . the Isles of Greece . . .
   And Aphrodite rising
From the Acropolis." . . . "You mean," said Fothergil, "from the Aegean!"
"It is all one," said Hermione, "the point is that
   I see her rising!"

Then Color spoke to them . . .
"As that toe moves," said Ravenswood Wimble, "I
   see the heavens
Turned into one vast Kaleidoscope . . . all the stars
   and moons
Dance through my soul like flakes of colored glass!"
Then waved the toe called Life, and as with one
   accord each of the company
Leapt gasping to his or her feet, as the case might be,

And cried: "I feel! I feel! I feel! I feel the Cosmic Urge!"

Then moved the toe called Italy,
And Fothergil Finch remarked: "Roses . . .
   roses . . . roses . . .
Onions and roses . . . roses are onions, and onions pigs . . .
And pigs are beautiful" . . .
And then the serious thinkers cried as one:
"Ah! Pigs are Beautiful!"
"Ah, Italy; oh, Italy!" cried Fothy Finch,
"Oh, never cease to move . . . Italy . . .
garlic . . . Venice . . .
Oh, bind my brows with garlic, lovely land, and
   turn me loose!"
And as the toe called Italy still moved
The little groups made it into a chant, and sang:
"Oh, bind my brows with garlic, love, and turn me loose!"

        * * *

"Hermione," I asked her afterward,
"Did you really see and feel anything when those
   educated toes wiggled?"
"How can you ask?" she said, very up-stagey.
"Hermione," I said, "we are old enough friends by
   this time, so we can deal frankly with one
   another. Tell me on the square . . . did you
   get it?"
"You are blaspheming at the shrink of Art!" she said.
"Hermione! You are dodging!"
"Did you notice," she said irrelevantly, "the nail
   polish she was using?
"It's QUITE the latest thing! For finger nails, too,

you know. That delicate rose pink, with just
the touch of creaminess in it! It's the creamy
tint that's new, you know. Isn't it simply
wonderful?"

KULTUR, AND THINGS

Do you know, Kultur isn't the same thing at
all as culture . . . FANCY!

When we took it up -- Kultur, I mean yes, --
we took it up in quite a serious way the other
evening -- our Little Group of Serious Thinkers, you
know -- and threshed it out thoroughly -- we hadn't
the slightest idea that it would lead us straight to
Nietzsche and -- and, well, all those people like that,
if you get what I mean. Though, of course, as the
man who spoke to us -- he was the LOVELIEST person!
 -- spoke in German, we may have missed some of
the finer shades.

Oh, yes, I had German in high school . . . really,
I was quite proficient . . . although, of course,
it's such a GUTTURAL kind of language -- don't you
think? -- that one wonders how they EVER sing it.
And then, the verbs! . . . but I had Latin verbs
about the same time, you know . . . and really,
isn't it surprising how some of those foreign languages
seem to RUN to verbs, if you get what I mean?

It seems it was the Germans who invented the Superman . . . and I suppose we must be grateful to them for that, no matter what they may have done with him after they invented him. . . .

I used to be quite taken with the Superman, you know. . . . Really, I didn't recognize how dangerous he might become. . . .

I didn't know he was German at all when we took him up. . . .

Have you read anything about the Blond Beast?

I felt rather attracted toward him for a long time myself . . . until lately. . . . But the attraction passed. . . . I'm not brunette, you know, at all. . . . Likely that's why I lost interest in him. . . .

Aren't affinities between people of different complexion simply WONDERFUL!

It makes me wonder if the Eugenists can be right after all!

Fothergil Finch says that's where the Eugenists fall down. . . . He says they don't take account of Affinities at all.

Sometimes one finds it very puzzling -- doesn't one? -- the way these modern causes and movements seem to contradict one another!

But if one is in tune with the Cosmic All these little inconsistencies don't matter.

The Cosmic All! . . . WHAT would we do without it?

How do you suppose people ever got along a generation or two ago before the Cosmos and all that sort of thing was discovered?

I've often thought about it . . . and of what life must have been like in those days! As Emerson . . . or WAS it Emerson? . . . says in one of his poems: "Better a year of Europe than a cycle of Cathay!"

That's what Fothy Finch says he always feels about Brooklyn . . . though I WILL say this for Brooklyn -- the first girl I saw with courage enough to wear one of those ankle watches on the street lived in Brooklyn.

But don't you think Brooklyn people are rather LIKE that . . . go to the latest things in dress, you know, in an EXTREME sort of way, so that people won't suspect they live in Brooklyn?

THE SPIRIT OF CHRISTMAS

ISN'T the Christmas festival just simply WONDERFUL?

For days beforehand I feel so uplifted -- so
well, OTHER-WORLDLY -- if you know what I mean.

Isn't it just dreadful that any MATERIAL
considerations have to spoil such a sacred time?

It does seem to me that somehow we might free
ourselves of WORLDLINESS and GREEDINESS and just
rise to the spiritual significance of the day. If only
we could!

And what a blessing it would be to the poor, tired
shop girls if we could!

Though, of course, they, the shop girls, I mean,
must be upheld even in their weariest moments by
the thought that they are helping on the beautiful
impulse of giving!

When they reflect that every article they sell is
to be a gift from one thoughtful and loving heart
to another they must forget the mere fatigue of the
flesh and just feel the stimulus, the inspiration, the
vibration!

There are gifts, I admit, that haven't the divine
spark of love to hallow them, but after all there
aren't so many of that sort. Love one another is

the spirit of Christmas -- and it prevails, whatever
the skeptics say to the contrary. And though
it's a pity there has to be a MATERIAL side to
Christmas at all, it's so comforting, so ennobling
to realize that back of the material gifts is Brotherly
Love.

It quite reassures one about the state of the world;
it certainly isn't getting worse with Brotherly Love
and the Spirit of Giving animating everybody.

Of course, Christmas giving IS a problem sometimes.
It is SO embarrassing when somebody you'd
forgotten entirely sends you a present.

I always buy several extra things just for that
emergency. Then, when an unexpected gift arrives,
I can rush off a return gift so promptly that
nobody'd ever DREAM I hadn't meant to send it all
along.

And I always buy things I'd like to have myself,
so that if they aren't needed for unexpected people
they're still not wasted.

With all my spirituality, I have a practical side,
you see.

All well BALANCED natures have both the spiritual
and the practical side. It's so essential, nowadays,
to be well balanced, and it's a great relief to me to
find I CAN be practical. It saves me a lot of trouble,
too, especially about this problem of Christmas giving.

I know the value of material things, for instance.
And I never waste money giving more expensive
presents to my friends than I receive from them.
That's one of the advantages of having a well
balanced nature, a PRACTICAL side.

And, anyway, the value of a gift is not in the
COST of it. Quite cheap things, when they represent
true thought and affection, are above rubies.

Mamma and Papa are going to get me a pearl
necklace, just to circle the throat, but beautifully
matched pearl. I wouldn't care for an
ostentatiously long string of pearls anyway.

Poor, dear Papa says he really can't afford it --
with times so hard, and those dear, pathetic
Europeans on everybody's hands, you know -- but
Mamma made him understand how necessary BEAUTY is
to me, and he finally gave in.

Isn't it just WONDERFUL how love rules us all at
Christmas time?

POOR DEAR MAMA AND FOTHERGIL FINCH

(Hermione's Boswell Loquitur)

HERMIONE'S mother, who has figured so
often as "Poor dear Mama" in these
pages, has come out definitely for Suffrage.

Someone told her that there was an alliance between
the liquor interests and the anti-Suffagists and she
believed it, and it shocked her.

Since the activities of her daughter have brought
her into contact with Modern Though her life has
been chiefly passed in one or another of three
phases: She has been shocked, she is being
shocked, or she fears that she is about to be shocked.

She is nearing fifty and rather stout, though her
figure is still not bad. She has an abundance of
chestnut hair, all her own, and naturally wave; her
hands are pretty, her feet are pretty, her face is pretty.
Her mouth is very small, almost disproportionately so,
and her eyes are very large and blue and very wide
open. She was intended for a placed
woman, but Hermione and Modern Thought
have made complete placidity impossible. She has
a fondness for rich brocades and pretty fans are
chocolate candy and big bowls of roses and comfortable
chairs. When she was Hermione's age

she used to do water color sketches; the outlines were penciled in by her drawing teacher, and she washed on the color very smoothly and neatly; but she heard a great many stories concerning the dissolute lives that artists lead and she gave it up. Nevertheless, she sometimes says: "Hermione comes by her interest in Art quite naturally."

Fothergil Finch and I called recently. Hermione was not in, and her mother suggested that we wait for her. Hermione's mother looks upon all of Hermione's friends with more or less suspicion, and she would not permit Fothergil in particular to be about the place for a moment if she were not obliged to; but she does not have the requisite sternness of character to resist her daughter. Fothergil, knowing that he is not approved of, scarcely does himself justice when Hermione's mother is present; although he endeavors to avoid offending her.

"Have you seen the play, 'Young America'?" asked Fothergil, searching for a safe topic of conversation.

A little ripple of alarm immediately ruffled the lakeblue innocence of her eyes.

"If it is a Problem Play, I have not," she said, "I consider such things dangerous."

"But it isn't, you know," said Fothergil eagerly. It's a -- a -- it's a perfectly NICE play. It's about a dog!"

"About a dog!" Her eyebrows went up, and her mouth rounded itself with the conviction that no perfectly nice play could possibly be about a dog. "I think that is dreadfully Coarse!" she said.

"But it isn't," protested Fothergil. "It's just the SORT of thing you'd like."

"Indeed!" She felt slightly insulted at his assumption of what she would like, and dismissed the subject with a wave of her pretty hand. Fothergil tried again.

"I hope," he said ingratiatingly, "that you haven't been bothered by mosquitoes." She looked a bit frightened, but said nothing, and he dashed on determinedly. "You know, this is a new variety of mosquitoes we've been having this year. Most of them have stripes on their legs, you know, but these have black legs this year. But maybe you haven't noticed -- -- "

He stopped in midcareer. The preposterous idea that she could be interested in examining the legs of mosquitoes had too evidently outraged Hermione's mother. Fothergil, flushed and embarrassed, tried to make it better and made it worse.

"Maybe you haven't noticed their -- er -- limbs," said Fothergil.

"I have not," she murmured.

Fothergil desperately persevered.

"We don't see so much as we used to of --
of -- -- " (I am sure he didn't know he was
going to finish the sentence when he began it, but
he plunged ahead) -- "of the Queen Anne style of
architecture."

With visible relief, and yet with a lurking suspicion,
she assented. And Fothergil, feeling himself
on safe ground at last, went on:

"Don't you think she was one of the most interesting
queens in English history -- Queen Anne?
Do you remember the anecdote -- -- ?

But she checked him, frightened again:

"I do not wish to hear it, Mr. Finch," she said.

"But," said Fothergil, "She was a most unexceptional
Queen -- not like, er -- not like -- well,
Cleopatra, you know, or any of those bad ones."

Hermione's mother was silent, but it was apparent
that she feared the talk was about to veer toward
Cleopatra.

"When I was a girl," she said, "the lives of
queens were considered rather dangerous reading
for young women. You need not go into details,
please."

I couldn't stand it any more myself. "If you'll just tell Hermione I called," I said, edging toward the door. Fothergil, however, stuck it out. In the frenzy of embarrassment he must have lost his head completely. For as I left I heard him beginning:

"Did you read the story in the papers today of the man who killed his wife? Crimes of passion are becoming more and more frequent...."

PRISON REFORM AND POISE

AREN'T you just crazy about prison reform?

The most wonderful man talked to us -- to our Little Group of Advanced Thinkers, you know -- about it the other evening.

It made me feel that I'd be willing to do anything, simply ANYTHING! -- to help those poor, unfortunate convicts. Collect money, you know, or give talks, or read books about them, or make any other sacrifice.

Even get them jobs. One ought to help them to start over again, you know.

Though as for hiring one of them myself, or

rather getting Papa to -- well, really, you know, one must draw the line somewhere!

But it's a perfectly fascinating subject to take up, prison reform is.

It gives one such a sense of brotherhood -- and of service -- it's so broadening, don't you think? -- taking up things like that?

And one must be broad. I ask myself every night before I go to bed: "Have I been BROAD today? Or have I failed?"

Though, of course, one can be TOO broad, don't you think?

What I mean is, one must not be so broad that one loses one's poise in the midst of things.

Poise! That is what this age needs!

I suppose you've heard wide-brimmed hats are coming in again?

AN EXAMPLE OF PSYCHIC POWER

HAVE you thought deeply concerning the Persistence of Personal Identity?

We took it up the other evening -- our

little group, you know -- in quite a thorough way --
devoted an entire evening to it.

You see, there's a theory that after Evolution has
evolved just as far as it possibly can, everything
will go to smash, but then Evolution will start all
over again. And everything that has happened before will happen again.

Only the question is whether the people to whom
it is happening again will know whether they
are the same people to whom it has happened
before.

That's where the question of Persistence of
Personal Identity comes in. FRIGHTFULLY
fascinating, isn't it?

For my part I'd just as soon not be reincarnated
as to be reincarnated and not know anything about
it, wouldn't you?

Of course, one's Subliminal Consciousness might
know about it, and give one intimations.

I've had intimations like that myself -- really!

I'm dreadfully psychic, you know.

Sometimes I quite startle people with my psychic
power.

Fothergil Finch was here the other evening --

you know fothergil Finch, the poet, don't you? --
and I astounded him utterly by reading his inmost
thoughts.

He had just finished reading one of his poems --
a vers libre poem, you know; all about Strength and
Virility, and that sort of thing. Fothergil is just
simply fascinated by Strength and Virility, though
you never would think it to look at him -- he is so --
so -- well, if you get what I mean you'd think to
look at him that he'd be writing about violets instead
of cave men.

"Fothy," I said, when he had finished reading
the poem, "I know what you are thinking -- what
you are feeling!"

"What?" he said.

"You're thinking," I said, 'how WONDERFUL a
thing is the Cosmic Urge!"

Thoughts come to me just like that -- leap to me --
right out of nowhere, so to speak.

Fothy was staggered; he actually turned pale;
for a minute or two he could scarcely speak. There
had been scarcely a WORD about Cosmic Urge in
the poem, you know; he'd hardly mentioned it.

"It is wonderful," he said, when we got over the
shock; "wonderful to be understood!" And you
know, really -- poor dear! -- so many people don't

understand Fothy at all. Nor what he writes, either.

But the strangest thing was -- I wish I could make you understand how positively EERIE it makes me feel -- that just the instant before he said, "It is wonderful to be understood!" I knew he was going to say it. I got that psychically, too!

"Fothy," I said, "It is absolutely WEIRD -- I eavesdropped on your brain the second time!"

"Wonderful!" he said, "but the still more wonderful thing would be -- -- "

And before he could finish the sentence it happened the THIRD time! I interrupted and finished it for him.

"The still more wonderful thing would be," I said, "if it were NOT so."

"Heavens!" he cried, "this is getting positively ghostly."

And you know, it almost was. Not that I'm superstitious at all, you know, in the vulgar way. But in the dim room -- I always have just candlelight in the drawing-room -- it fits in with my more reflective moods, somehow -- I believe one must suit one's environment to one's mood, don't you? -- in the dim room, all those thoughts flying back and forty between my brain and his gave me a positively creepy feeling. And Fothy was so shaken I had to give

him a drink of Papa's Scotch before he went out
into the night.

SOME BEAUTIFUL THOUGHTS

(Fothergil Finch, the Vers Libre Bard)

OH, the Beautiful Mud! I always leave it on
my boots. It is sacred to me. Because in
it are the souls of lilies!

The Hog should be a sacred beast. Hogs are
Beautiful! They are close to the Mire! Oh, to be
a Swine!

What is more eloquent than a Sneeze? The
Sneeze is the protest of the Free Spirit against the
Smug Citizen who never exposes himself to a cold.
Oh, Beautiful Sneezes! Oh, to make my life one
loud explosive Sneeze in the face of Conventionality!

What is so free, so untrammeled, so ungyved, so
unconventional, as an Influenza Germ? From
throat to throat it floats, full of the spirit of true
democratic brotherhood, making the masses equal
with the classes, careless, winged ungyved! Oh,
the Beautiful Germ! Oh, to be an Influenza Germ!

What is so naive as a Hiccough! Oh, to be ingenuous,

unspoiled, beautiful, barbaric! Oh, the
hiccoughs, the beautiful hiccoughs, the hiccoughs
of Art uttered against the hurricane of time.

Bugs are Beautiful! Oh, the beautiful, sleek
slithery bugs. Oh, to be a water-bug of poesy skipping
across the flood of oblivion! Oh, to be a Bug!

I went down to the waterfront where they sell
fish and there I saw a fisherman who had caught a
Dogfish, and he cursed, but I said to him, "Do not
curse the Dogfish! The Dogfish is Symbolical! The
Dogfish is beautiful! Beautiful!"

Oh, the lovely Garbage Scows! I went down the
bay, and there I saw them dump the Garbage Scows!
I said to the man who sailed my boat: "What does
the Garbage Scow MEAN to you?" He was a
Philistine; he was Bourgeois; he was Smug; he was
Conventional, and he said: "A Garbage Scow means a
Garbage Scow to me!" But I said to him: "You
are Academic; you are Conservative! Garbage
Scows are lovely Symbols! Oh, my Argosies of
Dream! Oh, my beautiful Garbage Scows! Some
day even the Philistines of Benighted America will
see the Spiritual Significance of the Lovely Garbage
Scow!"

I found a Glue Factory, a Free Untrammeled
Glue Factory! I was expressing itself. It was
asserting its individuality. It was saying to the
Blind Complacent Pillars of Polite Society: "My
aroma is not your aroma, but my aroma is my

own!" Oh, the Courageous Glue Factory, the Free, Unfettered Glue Factory! A thousand Glue Factories, from Main to Oregon, are thus rebuking Class Prejudice and Bourgeois Smugness. Like Poets, like Prophets of the New Art, they stand, Glue Factory after Glue Factory, expressing their Egos, Being Themselves, undaunted, unshackled, strong, independent, virile! Oh, to be the Poet of the Super Glue Factory!

With violets in my hands I wandered to the wilds, and there I met a Buzzard. He was Being Himself! I wove a wreath of the violets and I crowned the Buzzard, and the Buzzard said, "Why do you crown me?" And I said, "Oh, Lovely Buzzard, are you not Being Yourself? Are you not rebuking the Trivial Conventionalities of our Organized Society? I know your Dream, O Buzzard! Accept this Crown of Violets from our little group!"

Come with me to the zoo, and I will bare our Souls to the Hyena, and the Hyena will commune with us, and we will know the meaning of Life! Oh, the lovely Hyena.

THE BOURGEOIS ELEMENT AND BACKGROUND

ISN'T it simply wonderful about D'Annunzio enlisting as a common soldier and digging trenches along with the Due D'Abruzzi and those other Italian poets? Or was it D'Abruzzi? Anyhow, it was one of those poets that were always talking about the Superman.

Although, I must say, one doesn't hear so much about the Superman these days, does one? The Superman is going out, you know.

One of my friends -- she's quite an advanced thinker, too, and belongs to our little group -- told me a year or so ago, "Hermione, I will NEVER marry until I find a Superman!"

"Of course, that is all right, my dear," I said to her, "but how about Genetics?"

Because, you know, the slogan of our little group -- that is, one of the slogans -- is "Genetics or Spinsterhood!"

It made her quite angry for some reason. She pursed her lips up and acted shocked.

"It is all very well, Hermione," she said, "to discuss Genetics in the ABSTRACT. But to connect the discussion with the marriage of a FRIEND is not, to my mind, the proper thing at all!"

Did you ever hear of anything more utterly inconsistent?

Oh, Consistency! Consistency! Isn't Consistency perfectly wonderful!

But that is always the way when it comes to a discussion of Sex. The Bourgeois Element are NEVER Fundamental and Thorough in their treatment of Sex, if you know what I mean.

And, as Fothergil Finch says, in this country we are NEARLY all Bourgeois.

We have not had enough Background for one thing.

If all the little groups the country over would take up the matter of Background in a serious way, something might be done about it, don't you think?

We must organize -- we who are the intellectual leaders, you know -- and start an effective propaganda for the purpose of obtaining more Background.

TAKING UP THE LIQUOR PROBLEM

WE'RE thinking of taking up the Liquor problem -- our little group, you know, -- in quite a serious way.

The Working Classes would be so much better off without liquor. And we who are the leaders in thought should set them an example.

So a number of us have decided to set our faces very sternly against drinking in public.

Of course, a cocktail or two and an occasional stinger, is something no one can well avoid taking, if one is dining out or having supper after the theater with one's own particular crowd.

But all the members of my own particular little group have entered into a solemn agreement not to take even so much as a cocktail or a glass of wine if any of the working classes happen to be about where they can see us and become corrupted by our example.

The Best People owe those sacrifices to the Masses, don't you think?

Of course, the waiters, and people like that, really belong to the working classes too, I suppose.

Hermione and Her Little Group of Serious Thinkers

But, as Fothergil Finch says, very often one
wouldn't know it. And who could expect a waiter
to be influenced one way or another by anything?
And it's the home life of the working classes that
counts, anyhow.

When we took up Sociology -- we gave several
evenings to Sociological Discussion, you know,
besides doing a lot of practical Welfare Work -- it
was impressed upon me very strongly that if one is to
do anything at all for the Masses one must first
SWEETEN their Home Life.

Though Papa made me stop poking around into
the horrid places where they live for fear I might
catch some dreadful disease.

And the people we visited weren't all that grateful.
So VERY OFTEN the Masses are not.

One dreadful woman, you know, claimed that
she couldn't keep her rooms -- she had two rooms,
and she cooked and washed and slept and sewed
in them and there were five in the family -- claimed
that she couldn't keep her rooms in any better shape
because they were so out of repair and the plumbing
was bad and the windows leaked and all that
sort of thing, you know, and one of the rooms was
ENTIRELY dark.

I preached the doctrine of fresh air and sunshine
and cleanliness to her, you know, and the imprudent

thing told me Papa owned the building and it wasn't true at all -- Papa only belonged to the company that owned the building. One can't do much for people who will not be truthful with one, can one?

Besides, it is the Silent Influence that counts more than arguments and visiting.

If one makes one's life what it should be Good will Radiate.

Vibrations from one's Ego will permeate all classes of society.

And that is the way we intend to make ourselves felt with regard to the Liquor Problem. We will inculcate abstemiousness by example.

Abstemiousness, Fothy Finch says, should be our motto, rather than Abstinence. We shall be QUITE careful not to identify ourselves with the MORE VULGAR aspects of the propaganda.

And of course at social functions in our private homes total abstinence is quite out of the question.

The working classes wouldn't get any example from our homes, anyone; for of course we never come into contact with them there.

But the working classes must be saved from themselves, even if all the employers of labor have to write out a list of just what they eat and drink and make them buy only those things. They simply MUST be saved.

Not that they'll appreciate it. They never do. If I were not an incorrigible idealist I would be inclined to give them up.

But someone must give up his life to leading them onward and upward. And who is there to do it if not we leaders of Modern Thought?

THE JAPANESE ARE WONDERFUL, IF YOU GET WHAT I MEAN

DON'T you just dote on the Japanese?

They're so esoteric -- and subtle and all that sort of thing, aren't they?

Just look at Buddhism and Shintoism, for instance. Could anything be more subtle and esoteric?

We've been taking them up -- our Little Group of Serious Thinkers, you know -- and they've wonderful, simply WONDERFUL!

Not, of course, that one would BE a Buddhist or

a Shintoist -- but it's broadening to the mind, don't
you think, to come in contact with the great
thought of -- of -- well, really of people like Shinto,
you know, and those other sages?

And how wonderfully artistic they are -- the
Japanese!

The new parasols are quite Japanese, you know.
Haven't you seen them?

I have three, for different costumes. One is
covered with embroidered Japanese crepe, and an-
other with martine silk.

But the one, I think that express ME the most
accurately -- the one that represents my individuality,
REALLY -- is made with gold spokes covered with
black Chantilly lace. Japanese shape, you know,
and French workmanship.

And one must strive to represent one's self if one
is to be honest.

One must put one's soul into one's environment.

Although Environment isn't what it used to be.
You don't hear Environment spoken of nearly as
often as you did.

Environment is going out.

But besides being so esoteric and exotic and artistic,

and all that sort of things, the Japanese are
wonderfully up to date, too.

Do you know, they actually have a battleship
named The Tango!

Have you thought deeply of Interstellar Communication?

It promises to be one of the great new problems.

The loveliest man talked to us about it the other
evening. "Interstellar Communication in Its Relation
to Recent Psychic Hypotheses" -- that's the title;
I wrote it down. I always take notes of a title like that.
It helps one to get to the heart of the matter.

Interstellar Communication is wonderful -- simply WONDERFUL!

We're going to take up Mars soon.

Mamma said to me only yesterday: "Hermione,
you SIMPLY MUST drop some of your serious subjects
during the hot weather."

"Mamma," I told her, "that was all very well in
your day -- to take things up and drop them at will.
But people didn't have a Social Conscience in those
times. We advanced thinkers owe a duty to the
race. We must grapple with things. We are not
content to frivol, I WILL take up Mars!"

And, you know, I don't have the temperament to
remain idle. My mind MUST be active. Sometimes

when I think how active my mind is, I wonder my
forehead isn't wrinkled.

And of course that would be a loss -- anything
is a loss that destroys Beauty.

For, after all, Beauty is what the world needs
more than anything else. It's a serious thought --
how far Use should be sacrificed to Beauty, and
Beauty to Use, isn't it?

You know that's why I can't join the suffragists.
I am one, of course, but the suffragist yellow is
such a HORRID color I simply CANNOT wear it.

SHE REFUSES TO GIVE UP THE COSMOS

WE'VE taken up Gertrude Stein -- our Little
Group of Serious Thinkers, you know --
and she's wonderful; simply WONDERFUL.

She Suggests the Inexpressible, you know.

Of course, she is a Pioneer. And with all
Pioneers -- don't you think -- the Reach is greater
than the Grasp.

Not that you can tell what she means.

But in the New Art, one doesn't have to mean

Hermione and Her Little Group of Serious Thinkers

things, does one? One strikes the chords, and the chords vibrate.

Aren't Vibrations just too perfectly lovely for anything?

The loveliest man talked to us the other night about World Movements and Cosmic Vibrations.

You see, every time the Cosmos vibrates it means a new World Movement.

And the Souls that are in Tune with the Cosmos are benefitted by these World Movements. The other souls will get harm out of them.

Frightfully interesting, isn't it? -- the Cosmos, I mean.

I have given so much thought to it! It has become almost an obsession to me.

Only the other evening I was thinking about it. And without realizing that I spoke aloud I said, "I simply could NOT DO WITHOUT the Cosmos!"

Mamma -- poor Mamma! -- she is so terribly unadvanced you know! -- Mama said: "Hermione, I do not know what the Cosmos is. But this I do know -- not another Sex Discussion or East Indian Swami will ever come into THIS house!"

"Mamma," I said to her, "I will NOT give up the Cosmos. It means everything to me; simply EVERYTHING!"

I am always firm with Mamma; it is kinder, in the long run, to be quite positive. But what I suffer at home from objections to the advanced movements nobody knows!

Nobody but the Leaders of Thought can dream what Martyrdom is!

Sacrifice! Sacrifice! That is the keynote of the Liberal Life!

Nearly every night before I go to bed I ask myself: "Have I shown the Sacrificial Spirit to day? Or have I FAILED?"

THE CAVE MAN

DON'T you think the primitive is just simply too fascinating for anything? We've all got it in us, you know, and it seems like nowadays the more cultured and advanced one is the more likely the primitives is to break out on one.

I have a strong strain of the primitive in me, you know.

I wouldn't take anything for it -- it's simply wonderful -- wonderful!

It comes over me so strong at times, the yearning

for the primitive does, that I just sit with a dreamy look on my face and murmur to myself: "ALONE, ALONE -- UNDER THE STARS! ALONE!"

Mamma overheard me saying that the other day and thought I had gone crazy, and she said: "for Heaven's sake, Hermione, what are you thinking about, and what do you want?"

"The stars," I murmured, scarcely knowing that I spoke aloud, "the stars and my Cave Man!"

Mamma was shocked -- she says for an unmarried woman to think of Cave Men is simply indelicate.

Mamma is not at all advanced, you know.

She's dear and sweet, but she doesn't believe in Trial Marriages at all.

And I must admit they shocked me when I first heard about them. But that was before I had taken up these things seriously.

"Mamma," I said to her, "it is no use for you to pretend to be shocked. I have a right to happiness. And happiness to me means being alone, under the stars, and walking barefoot and bareheaded in the dew."

"Alone with a Cave Man!" she said. And then she cried.

Tears! -- that is so like the old-fashioned woman!

"Mamma," I said, kindly, but firmly, "If it is my destiny to be kidnaped by a Cave Man and taken into the waste places, under the stars, can I avoid it?"

She said I could at least be respectable, and that I was acting like I WANTED to be kidnaped.

And, you know, at times I do feel as if that might be my fate, "really. I am so psychic, you know, and psychics feel their fate coming on quicker than most people.

I told Mamma that I felt every woman had a right to choose the father of her own children, and she was shocked again. And then she wanted to know what being kidnaped by a Cave Man had to do with choosing the father of one's own children, and how did I know but these Cave Men kidnaped a different woman every year?

But I settled her.

"Mamma," I said, "you are NOT advanced, and so I cannot argue with you. You wouldn't understand. But if I AM primitive -- and I feel that I am -- whose fault is it? Who did I inherit it from?"

She couldn't say anything to that. She didn't like to own that I inherited it from her. And she knew if she blamed it onto Papa I would ask her how she DARED to deny me a primitive man when she had married one herself.

Finally she quit crying and said, pressing her
lips together: "Hermione, do you KNOW any of
those Cave Men?"

But I refused to answer. I went to my room.

Dissension disturb's the soul's harmony.

One's subliminal consciousness must ever vibrate
in harmony with the Cosmic All.

I never fuss when a person disturbs me. I just
go into the Silences and vibrate there.

But I kept thinking: "DO I know any Cave Men?"

I Think I do -- one. He tries to conceal it. But
it's his secret. I'm sure.

He has the most luminous eyes!

Like a wolf's, you know, when it gallops across
the waste places -- under the stars, alone!

And the way he eats! I don't mean that he's
noisy, you know. But the way he crunched a chicken
bone the last time he dined with me was perfectly
WONDERFUL -- so nonchalant, you know, and loudly
and -- and -- well, primitive! I'm SURE he's one!

I wouldn't go autoing with him for anything --

unless, of course, he gave me one of those compelling
glances, like Cave Men do in the magazines, you know.
Then I'd know it was destiny and useless to resist.

THE LITTLE GROUP GIVES A PAGAN MASQUE

The Little Group gave a party
   And all of the gods were there,
From Thor to Miss Susan Astarte
   With doo-daddles gemming her hair,

Bill Baldur and Jane Aphrodite,
   Dick Vishnu and Benny O'Baal,
And Bacchus came on in a nightie
   With little pink snakes in the tail;

Latin, Phoenician and Hindu
   Norse and Egyptian and Chink....
Castor was watching his Twin do
   Stunts, with a brotherly wink....

Persephone swearing by Hades....
   A Norn and Sibylline Simp....
A Momus, who showed up to the ladies
   The latest Olympian limp.

Was Hermione present? By Crikey!
   (This Crikey's a Whitechapel joss)

Hermione and Her Little Group of Serious Thinkers

Our Hermy attended as Psyche --
   She siked and she got it across

And Fothergil Finch, rather gaumy
   With Cosmic cosmetics, was there,
But the Swami went just as the Swami,
   After oiling the kinks in his hair.

I said to Hermione: "Goddess!
   You're graceful, you're Greek, you're a rose,
From the pinions that rise from your bodice
   To the raddle I note on your toes,

"And Fothergil, here, with his censer,
   And his little cheeks crimson as beets,
Your acolyte, perfume-dispenser,
   Is sweet as a page out of Keats,

"But tell me, my Dea -- my Psyche! --
   (With your wings outspread as to race
With that swift and acephalous Nike
   Who lost her bean somewhere in Thrace) --

"My Thea -- my classical pigeon! --
   Is not your Sincerity shocked
By this giddy revue of religion? . . .
   Are none of these gods being mocked? . . .

"In the regions unknowable -- Thea! --
   Where the noumenon chumbs with the Nous,
Where the Idol gets hep to Idea,
   And pythagoras ogles a Goose,

"In the heavens of Brahm and Osiris,
   Are they peeved with this revel, I ask? . . .
Does Pluto like this, where his fire is? . . .
   What in hell do they think of this masque? . . .

"Where the deities, avid of Is-ness,
   Resurge from the Flivvers that Were,
While the wild Chaotical Whizness
   Gives place to a Cosmic Whir,

"Do they relish this josh of the josses?
   Do they lamp not the same with a grouch?
Are you stinging these gloomy Big Bosses
   To a keener, immortaler ouch?"

Hermione murmured: "How eerie!
   You are voicing my own Inner Mood!
Ah me! but the world is less dreary
   If one is but understood!

"And I thank you, I thank you, for rising
   To my personal point of view. . . .
I THANK you for SYMPATHIZING! . . .
   Dear man, how you always do!"

SYMPATHY

OF course we're out of town for the summer --
EVERYBODY'S out of town, now -- but

Hermione and Her Little Group of Serious Thinkers

I motor in once or twice a week to keep in
touch with some of my committees.

Sociological work, for instance, keeps right up
the year around.

Of course, it's not so interesting in the winter.
You see more striking contrasts in the winter, don't
you think?

A couple of girl cousins of mine from Cincinnati
have been here. They're interested in welfare work
of all sorts.

"Hermione," they said, "we want to see the
bread line."

"My dears," I said, "I don't mind showing it to
you, but it's nothing much to see in summer. It's
in the winter that it arouses one's deepest sympathies."

And one must keep one's sympathies aroused.
Often I say to myself at night: "Have I been
sympathetic today, or have I FAILED?"

Mamma often lacks sympathy. She objects to
having me reopen my Salon this winter.

"Hermione," she said, "I don't mind the subjects
you take up -- or the people you take up with -- if
you only take them up one at a time. And I am
glad when your own little group meets here, be-
cause it keeps you at home. But I will NOT have

all the different kinds of freaks here at the SAME TIME, sitting around discussing free love and sex education."

I was indignant. "Mamma," I said, "what right have you to say they would discuss that all the time?"

"Because," she said, "I have noticed that no matter whether they start with sociology or psychology, they always get around to Sex in the end."

Isn't it funny about pure-minded people? -- in the generation before this anything that shocked a pure-minded person like Mamma was sure to be bad.

But now its only the evil-minded people who ever get shocked at all, it seems.

The really PUREST of the pure-minded people don't get shocked by anything at all these days.

I think Mamma is either getting purer-minded all the time or is losing some of it -- I can't tell which -- for she isn't shocked as easily as she was a few months ago.

But I got a shock myself recently.

I found out that plants have Sex, you know.

Just think of it -- carrots, onion, turnips, potatoes, and everything!

Isn't it frightful to think that this agitation has
spread to the vegetable kingdom?

I vowed I would never eat another potato as
long as I lived!

And, after all, what GOOD does it do -- letting the
vegetable kingdom have Sex, I mean?

Even a good thing, you know, can be carried too far.

"Mamma," I told her, "you are hopelessly behind
the times. Sex is a Great Fact. Someone must
discuss it. And who but the Leaders of Thought
are worthy to?"

I intend to say nothing more about it now -- but
when the time comes I WILL reopen my Salon.

And as far as talking about Sex is concerned --
the right sort of mind will get GOOD out of it, and
the wrong sort will get HARM.

I don't really LIKE discussions of Sex any more
than Mamma does. No really nice girl does.

But we advanced thinkers owe a duty to the race.

Not that the race is grateful. Especially the
lower classes.

It was only last week that I was endeavoring to

introduce the cook to some advanced ideas -- for her
own good, you know, and because one owes a spiritual
duty to one's servants -- and she got angry and gave notice.

The servant problem is frightful. It will have to
be taken seriously.

BLOUSES, BURGARS AND BUTTERMILK

SOME of us -- Our Little Group of Advanced
Thinkers, you know -- are going in for Bulgarian
buttermilk.

It came in about the time the Bulgarian blouses
did -- there was a war over there somewhere, you
know, before this big war, that made it fashionable.

But the blouses went out, and the buttermilk
stayed in.

It seems there's a Bulgarian by the name of
Metchnikoff in Paris who sits down and designs
these things -- the buttermilk, you know, not the
blouses.

Isn't science wonderful -- simply WONDERFUL!

We're going to take up Metchnikoff in a serious way.

Hermione and Her Little Group of Serious Thinkers

You know what he aims to do is to lengthen life.

The question is: "Should life be lengthened?
Or should it not?

The Leaders of Thought will have to thresh that
out soon.

The question of old age is a subtle one, isn't it?

And it's very typical of our times, don't you think,
that we should discuss the problems of old age?

Other epochs have done it, of course, but not
optimistically.

The question enters into everything -- even millinery.

I'm having the loveliest hat adapted from a
French model -- to wear with my lingerie costumes,
you know -- a wide-brimmed black lace with a black
velvet crown.

It's only recently that young women could afford
to wear black, even when it was becoming. When
Mamma was young it was a sign that youth was
past.

And nowadays, age doesn't matter so much one
way or another. A person is the age one FEELS,
you know.

Have you thought deeply on Hypnagogic

Illusions? We're planning to take them up.

TWILIGHT SLEEP

HAVE you read anything about the Twilight Sleep yet? It's wonderful; simply WONDERFUL!

The loveliest man told our little group all about it -- just the other evening.

"Hermione," said Mamma, "I will NOT have you taking up any more subjects of that Easy Indian character. No Swami shall ever enter this house again!"

"Mamma," I said to her, "you are hopelessly unadvanced., It has nothing whatever to do with Going into the Silences or Swamis. It's entirely scientific and not psychic at all. And if it were psychic, what then?"

"No Swami," said Mamma, even more stubbornly, "shall ever darken my door again!"

Poor, dear, stupid Mamma! She gets things so mixed!

"As far as Swamis are concerned," I told her, "the debt we owe to them in incalculable. Where, for instance, would we have ever heard of Karma if it had not been for the Swamis?"

She couldn't answer; she just looked stubborn; unadvanced people always look stubborn and glare.

"Where," I said, "did we get the Vedantas and Vegetarianism and Alternate Breathing from?"

She couldn't say a word. She just pouted.

"Who taught us," I said, "Transmigration of Souls and Vibrations?"

She broke down and cried.

"Hermione," she said, "I simply HATE howdahs and cobras and swastikas and all those Oriental things!"

Mamma has no idea whatever of logic. She is a typical old-fashioned woman.

"Mamma," I said, "cry as much as you like. You shall not disturb MY inner Harmony! I will not permit you to. And my mind is made up. I will take up the Twilight Sleep in a serious way!"

That settled it, too.

Have you noticed, there's been just a hint of autumn in the air these last few days?

Have you seen the new styles for autumn? They

are wonderful; simply WONDERFUL!

INTUITION

IN spite of all we've done for them -- by we I
mean the serious thinkers of the world -- some
people are so frightfully uncultured!

A girl asked me the other day -- and the surprising
thing about it, too, is that she belonged to our
own Little Group of Advanced Thinkers -- she asked
me: "Hermione, don't you just done on Rubaiyat's
poetry?"

For a moment I couldn't think who she meant at all.

"He's not an American, is he?" I said.

"Oh, no," she said, "he's some sort of an Oriental."

"It isn't Rubaiyat you're thinking of, my dear,"
I told her. It's Rabindranath. Rabindranath
Something-or-other, that new man -- he's wonderful,
 my dear, simply wonderful."

And then she quoted some of it and -- the idea
is too absurd for anything, but what do you sup-
pose it was?

Omar Khayyam -- imagine!

Hermione and Her Little Group of Serious Thinkers

And really, you know, it's been years since anybody quoted Omar Khayyam; he's QUITE gone out, you know!

Even the question whether he was moral doesn't attract any attention any more. Although as far as that is concerned, the pure mind will get purity out of him and the impure mind will get impurity. Honi sit qui -- what is the rest of it? Oh, you know -- it's Latin -- what the Romans used to say about Caesar's wife and her continual suspicions.

My, how a suspicious wife can handicap a man!

But, of course, as women get more and more advanced, and know about the lives men lead, they are finding out that the suspicions were justified.

Their intuitions told them so all the time.

I have a lot of intuition myself -- the moment a man comes I judge him in spite of myself.

First impressions always last with me, too.

You know, I'm very psychic.

Sometimes I am almost frightened when I think of the things my intuition would tell me if I allowed it to roam at will, so to speak, among my friends and acquaintances.

But I restrain it. One must, you know. The

loveliest man gave us such an interesting talk on
self-restraint the other evening.

And now I always ask myself the last thing before I go to bed at night: "Have I restrained myself today? Or have I failed?"

There is no real culture without restraint, you know.

That's where the English are so superior, don't
you think?

I met the loveliest Englishman the other evening.
The moment I saw him I said to myself he
was one of the aristocracy. Other people have
noses like theirs, of course, but it is only the
English aristocracy who can CARRY that kind of a nose.

And my intuition was correct -- there are only
five lives between him and a title, and one of those
is a polo player and another is at the front.

Someone told me his family were paying him
not to go home, but what they think the poor man
would do if he were in England I don't know,
because they don't duel there, you know. If they
dueled there, of course, he might dispose of all
five lives.

Don't you think those old European families are
so, so -- well, so ROMANTIC somehow?

STIMULATING INFLUENCES

SCIENCE and philanthropy should go hand in hand -- two hearts that beat as one, if you know what I mean, and all that sort of thing.

And they do, too. We were discussing it the other evening -- our Little Group of Serious Thinkers, you know -- and we decided that what philanthropy owes to science is made up by what science owes to philanthropy.

Isn't it wonderful how things balance like that?

There's the Twilight Sleep and the Mother-Teacher Idea, for instance.

Our little group are thinking of starting a propaganda to urge ALL Teachers to be Mothers.

And, of course, a lot of them might object -- but along comes the Twilight Sleep and takes away all POSSIBLE objections.

And along comes Philanthropy to put the Twilight Sleep within the reach of all -- at least, we hope it will -- and we're going to take the matter up with some of the Philanthropists right away.

Isn't it just simply WONDERFUL how Modern Thought brings subjects like that together?

Of course, even Modern Thought couldn't do it, unless the subjects belonged together, anyhow, could it? Unless they were -- er -- er -- --

Well, you know, Affinities. Though I don't care much for the word.

Affinities have quite gone out, you know. You don't hear much about Affinities this autumn.

Nor Soul Mates, either, for that matter.

Though I always will say there's an IDEA behind all the talk about them.

Isn't it odd about things that way -- how Ideas come and go, you know, and become quite old-fashioned, and yet all the time have a QUITE profound Idea back of them?

There's Cubist and Futurist Art, for instance -- one doesn't hear nearly so much about them now, though everyone admitted there was an Idea behind them.

Of course, no one knew what the Idea MEANT.

But it was stimulating.

And why should an Idea have to MEAN anything if it is STIMULATING?

Hermione and Her Little Group of Serious Thinkers

Stimulation! Stimulation! That is the secret
of Modern Life!

One should be receptive to Stimulation -- one
should strive to Stimulate!

One owes it to the Masses to Stimulate! It is
the DUTY of the leaders of Advanced Thought!

Nearly every night before I go to bed I ask myself,
"Have I been a Stimulating Influence today?
Or have I failed?"

Fothergil Finch says I Stimulate HIM!

Poor, dear man! -- he's becoming quite -- quite --
well, er -- er -- TOO encouraged, if you know what I mean.

Yes, that is the way with poets.

I doubt if ANY poet ever understood a purely
Platonic Friendship.

I gave him a long, long look last evening and said,
"Fothergil, CAN you keep on the Platonic Plane?"

He only said, "Alas! The Platonic Plane!"

I hope he can. I need him for my Salon.

I'm having the entire ground floor of the house
done over for that, you know, and I may reopen it
any time now!

POLITICS

I'M thinking of taking up politics in a practical way.

I've never been an active suffragist, you know, on account of that horrid yellow color on the banners and things.

But one must sacrifice Ideals of Beauty to Ideals of Usefulness, mustn't one?

And politics is fascinating; simply FASCINATING!

Going about and organizing working girls, you know, and seeing Corrupt Bosses and enlisting them for Moral Causes, and making one's self felt as a Force -- could one make one's self more Utile?

More spiritually Utile?

Utility! That is what our Leaders of Thought need to develop!

Nearly every night before I go to bed I say to myself: "Have I been Utile today? Or have I FAILED?"

Politics, practical politics, will be such an outlet

for my personality, too.

And when I reopen my Salon I can make it count
for the Cause, too.

We are going to give an evening soon -- our
Group of Advanced Thinkers, you know -- to a serious
and thorough study of political economy. They
say it's simply wonderful.

The loveliest woman talked to us the other evening.
She's a poet. When women have charge of
affairs, she said, Humanitarianism, Idealism and the
Poetic Spirit will rule in public life.

Won't that be lovely?

But we must be practical, and get the Bosses on
our side. They are simply horrid people socially
and ethically, you know. But there's something
frightfully fascinating about the idea of bearding
them in their dens with petitions and things.

Though how the idea of abolishing men altogether
will work out I don't know.

Some of the leaders of the Cause seem to want it.
I have no doubt that it could be done. Some plants and
insects have only the female sex, you know. And
maybe the human race will be that way one day.

Although, for my part, if they could only be
reformed I'd favor retaining men.

There's something about them so -- so -- well, so
MASCULINE somehow, if you know what I mean.

But I must hurry -- I have to do some shopping.

Clothes are a bore, aren't they?

HERMIONE ON PSYCHICAL RESEARCH

SPIRITUALISM is becoming quite the thing,
isn't it?

Dear Sir Oliver Lodge has been proving
some more things quite recently, you know. How
anyone could doubt a man with such a lovely head
and face I can't imagine.

Spiritualism and Spiritism are quite different, you
know. It has been a long time, really, since
Spiritualism was taken seriously.

Except by superstitious people, of course.

But Spiritism has come to stay. It has nothing
to do with superstition at all. It's part of Advanced
Thought -- quite scientific, you know, while
Spiritualism was just a fad.

And Spiritualism is somehow more -- well, er --

VULGAR if you get what I mean. The sort of people one cares to know well have dropped Spiritualism for Spiritism.

Though, of course, a ghost is a ghost, whether it is materialized by spiritualism or Spiritism.

I have been often told that I am naturally very clairvoyant -- if I were developed I would make a splendid medium. Mediums have seen shapes hovering around my head, and once when I was at school I did some automatic writing.

It was the strangest, easiest thing! I had a pencil in my hand and without thinking of anything in particular at all I just scribbled away, and what I wrote was, "When in the course of human events it becomes necessary; When in the course of human events it becomes necessary," over and over again.

I was quite startled, for the last thing I had been thinking of was an algebra examination, and not history at all. We had had our history examination days before.

I felt as if an unseen hand had reached out of the Silences and grasped mine!

Wasn't it weird?

And I know who it was, too. A distant relative of Mamma's on her father's side, by marriage, was one of the men who signed the Constitution of the

United States in Faneuil Hall, in Philadelphia, in 1776, and it was HIS spirit that was trying to deliver his message through me!

And only last year I came across a very similar case. Only this was stranger than mine, if anything. For it happened on a typewriter -- which proves that the veil between the two worlds must be very thin, doesn't it, if the spirits are taking up modern inventions?

It happened to one of Papa's stenographers. I had her up to the house to take notes for a report I was making to one of the sociological committees I was on then.

And she took the notes and put them into shape for me, but when she sent the report to me the back of one of the sheets was just full of one sentence written over and over again. She didn't know she'd included that sheet, of course.

It was so curious I asked her about it.

She looked a little queer and said that when she wasn't thinking of anything in particular, but just sitting before her typewriter and not working, she always wrote that sentence.

"It just comes into my head," she said, "and I write it."

"An occult force guides your fingers?" I asked.

"Yes, ma'am, that's it," she said.

Over and over and over again she had written, "Now is the time for all good men to come to the aid of the party."

And here is the eerie part of it -- it almost frightened me when I got it out of her! -- her father had been some sort of politician; a district leader, or something like that. And he was dead, and she had had to go to work.

But he was trying to deliver a message through her!

Isn't Psychical Research simply wonderful!

Not that I'd care to go in for any vulgar thing such as tin trumpets, you know, but -- --

Well, there's the Astral Body. That hasn't been vulgarized at all, if you get what I mean. Really, the Best People have them.

ENVOY

HERMIONE, THE DEATHLESS

She will not die! -- in Brainstorm Slum
  Fake, Nut and Freak Psychologist

Eternally shall buzz and hum,
   And Spook and Swami keep their tryst
   with Thinkers in a Mental Mist.
You threaten her with Night and Sorrow?
   Out of the Silences, I wist,
More Little Groups will rise tomorrow!

The lips of Patter ne'er are dumb,
   The Futile Mills shall grind their grist
Of sand from now till Kingdom Come;
   The Winds of Bunk are never whist.
   You scowl and shake an honest fist --
You threaten her with Night and Sorrow?
   Go slay one Pseudo-Scientist,
More Little Groups will rise tomorrow!

With Fudge to feed the Hungry Bum
   She plays the Girl Philanthropist --
Each pinchbeck, boy Millenium
   She swings, a Bangle, at her wrist --
   Blithe Parrot and Pert Egoist,
You threaten her with Night and Sorrow?
   Hermiones will aye persist!
More Little Groups will rise tomorrow!

She, whom Prince Platitude has kissed,
   You threaten her with Night and Sorrow?
Slay her by thousands, friend -- but list:
   More Little Groups will rise tomorrow!

(I)

www.bookjungle.com *email: sales@bookjungle.com fax: 630-214-0564 mail: Book Jungle PO Box 2226 Champaign, IL 61825*

The Codes Of Hammurabi And Moses
W. W. Davies

QTY

The discovery of the Hammurabi Code is one of the greatest achievements of archaeology, and is of paramount interest, not only to the student of the Bible, but also to all those interested in ancient history...

Religion   **ISBN:** *1-59462-338-4*   Pages:132
MSRP $12.95

The Theory of Moral Sentiments
Adam Smith

QTY

This work from 1749. contains original theories of conscience amd moral judgment and it is the foundation for systemof morals.

Philosophy   **ISBN:** *1-59462-777-0*   Pages:536
MSRP $19.95

Jessica's First Prayer
Hesba Stretton

QTY

In a screened and secluded corner of one of the many railway-bridges which span the streets of London there could be seen a few years ago, from five o'clock every morning until half past eight, a tidily set-out coffee-stall, consisting of a trestle and board, upon which stood two large tin cans, with a small fire of charcoal burning under each so as to keep the coffee boiling during the early hours of the morning when the work-people were thronging into the city on their way to their daily toil...

Childrens   **ISBN:** *1-59462-373-2*   Pages:84
MSRP $9.95

My Life and Work
Henry Ford

QTY

Henry Ford revolutionized the world with his implementation of mass production for the Model T automobile. Gain valuable business insight into his life and work with his own auto-biography... "We have only started on our development of our country we have not as yet, with all our talk of wonderful progress, done more than scratch the surface. The progress has been wonderful enough but..."

Biographies/   **ISBN:** *1-59462-198-5*   Pages:300
MSRP $21.95

www.bookjungle.com *email: sales@bookjungle.com fax: 630-214-0564 mail: Book Jungle PO Box 2226 Champaign, IL 61825*

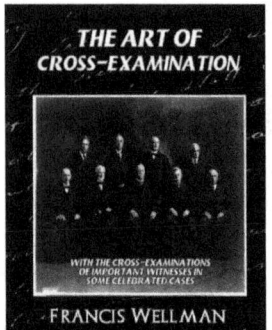

The Art of Cross-Examination
Francis Wellman

QTY

I presume it is the experience of every author, after his first book is published upon an important subject, to be almost overwhelmed with a wealth of ideas and illustrations which could readily have been included in his book, and which to his own mind, at least, seem to make a second edition inevitable. Such certainly was the case with me; and when the first edition had reached its sixth impression in five months, I rejoiced to learn that it seemed to my publishers that the book had met with a sufficiently favorable reception to justify a second and considerably enlarged edition. ..

Reference   ISBN: *1-59462-647-2*   Pages:412   MSRP *$19.95*

On the Duty of Civil Disobedience
Henry David Thoreau

QTY

Thoreau wrote his famous essay, On the Duty of Civil Disobedience, as a protest against an unjust but popular war and the immoral but popular institution of slave-owning. He did more than write—he declined to pay his taxes, and was hauled off to gaol in consequence. Who can say how much this refusal of his hastened the end of the war and of slavery ?

Law   ISBN: *1-59462-747-9*   Pages:48   MSRP *$7.45*

Dream Psychology Psychoanalysis for Beginners
Sigmund Freud

QTY

Sigmund Freud, born Sigismund Schlomo Freud (May 6, 1856 - September 23, 1939), was a Jewish-Austrian neurologist and psychiatrist who co-founded the psychoanalytic school of psychology. Freud is best known for his theories of the unconscious mind, especially involving the mechanism of repression; his redefinition of sexual desire as mobile and directed towards a wide variety of objects; and his therapeutic techniques, especially his understanding of transference in the therapeutic relationship and the presumed value of dreams as sources of insight into unconscious desires.

Psychology   ISBN: *1-59462-905-6*   Pages:196   MSRP *$15.45*

The Miracle of Right Thought
Orison Swett Marden

QTY

Believe with all of your heart that you will do what you were made to do. When the mind has once formed the habit of holding cheerful, happy, prosperous pictures, it will not be easy to form the opposite habit. It does not matter how improbable or how far away this realization may see, or how dark the prospects may be, if we visualize them as best we can, as vividly as possible, hold tenaciously to them and vigorously struggle to attain them, they will gradually become actualized, realized in the life. But a desire, a longing without endeavor, a yearning abandoned or held indifferently will vanish without realization.

Self Help   ISBN: *1-59462-644-8*   Pages:360   MSRP *$25.45*

www.bookjungle.com email: sales@bookjungle.com fax: 630-214-0564 mail: Book Jungle PO Box 2226 Champaign, IL 61825

QTY

	Title	ISBN	Price
☐	**The Rosicrucian Cosmo-Conception Mystic Christianity** by *Max Heindel*	ISBN: 1-59462-188-8	$38.95

The Rosicrucian Cosmo-conception is not dogmatic, neither does it appeal to any other authority than the reason of the student. It is: not controversial, but is: sent forth in the, hope that it may help to clear...
New Age/Religion Pages 646

☐ **Abandonment To Divine Providence** by *Jean-Pierre de Caussade* ISBN: 1-59462-228-0 $25.95
"The Rev. Jean Pierre de Caussade was one of the most remarkable spiritual writers of the Society of Jesus in France in the 18th Century. His death took place at Toulouse in 1751. His works have gone through many editions and have been republished...
Inspirational/Religion Pages 400

☐ **Mental Chemistry** by *Charles Haanel* ISBN: 1-59462-192-6 $23.95
Mental Chemistry allows the change of material conditions by combining and appropriately utilizing the power of the mind. Much like applied chemistry creates something new and unique out of careful combinations of chemicals the mastery of mental chemistry...
New Age Pages 354

☐ **The Letters of Robert Browning and Elizabeth Barret Barrett 1845-1846 vol II** ISBN: 1-59462-193-4 $35.95
by *Robert Browning* and *Elizabeth Barrett*
Biographies Pages 596

☐ **Gleanings In Genesis (volume I)** by *Arthur W. Pink* ISBN: 1-59462-130-6 $27.45
Appropriately has Genesis been termed "the seed plot of the Bible" for in it we have, in germ form, almost all of the great doctrines which are afterwards fully developed in the books of Scripture which follow...
Religion/Inspirational Pages 420

☐ **The Master Key** by *L. W. de Laurence* ISBN: 1-59462-001-6 $30.95
In no branch of human knowledge has there been a more lively increase of the spirit of research during the past few years than in the study of Psychology, Concentration and Mental Discipline. The requests for authentic lessons in Thought Control, Mental Discipline and...
New Age/Business Pages 422

☐ **The Lesser Key Of Solomon Goetia** by *L. W. de Laurence* ISBN: 1-59462-092-X $9.95
This translation of the first book of the "Lernegton" which is now for the first time made accessible to students of Talismanic Magic was done, after careful collation and edition, from numerous Ancient Manuscripts in Hebrew, Latin, and French...
New Age/Occult Pages 92

☐ **Rubaiyat Of Omar Khayyam** by *Edward Fitzgerald* ISBN: 1-59462-332-5 $13.95
Edward Fitzgerald, whom the world has already learned, in spite of his own efforts to remain within the shadow of anonymity, to look upon as one of the rarest poets of the century, was born at Bredfield, in Suffolk, on the 31st of March, 1809. He was the third son of John Purcell...
Music Pages 172

☐ **Ancient Law** by *Henry Maine* ISBN: 1-59462-128-4 $29.95
The chief object of the following pages is to indicate some of the earliest ideas of mankind, as they are reflected in Ancient Law, and to point out the relation of those ideas to modern thought.
Religion/History Pages 452

☐ **Far-Away Stories** by *William J. Locke* ISBN: 1-59462-129-2 $19.45
"Good wine needs no bush, but a collection of mixed vintages does. And this book is just such a collection. Some of the stories I do not want to remain buried for ever in the museum files of dead magazine-numbers an author's not unpardonable vanity..."
Fiction Pages 272

☐ **Life of David Crockett** by *David Crockett* ISBN: 1-59462-250-7 $27.45
"Colonel David Crockett was one of the most remarkable men of the times in which he lived. Born in humble life, but gifted with a strong will, an indomitable courage, and unremitting perseverance...
Biographies/New Age Pages 424

☐ **Lip-Reading** by *Edward Nitchie* ISBN: 1-59462-206-X $25.95
Edward B. Nitchie, founder of the New York School for the Hard of Hearing, now the Nitchie School of Lip-Reading, Inc, wrote "LIP-READING Principles and Practice". The development and perfecting of this meritorious work on lip-reading was an undertaking...
How-to Pages 400

☐ **A Handbook of Suggestive Therapeutics, Applied Hypnotism, Psychic Science** ISBN: 1-59462-214-0 $24.95
by *Henry Munro*
Health/New Age/Health/Self-help Pages 376

☐ **A Doll's House: and Two Other Plays** by *Henrik Ibsen* ISBN: 1-59462-112-8 $19.95
Henrik Ibsen created this classic when in revolutionary 1848 Rome. Introducing some striking concepts in playwriting for the realist genre, this play has been studied the world over.
Fiction/Classics/Plays 308

☐ **The Light of Asia** by *sir Edwin Arnold* ISBN: 1-59462-204-3 $13.95
In this poetic masterpiece, Edwin Arnold describes the life and teachings of Buddha. The man who was to become known as Buddha to the world was born as Prince Gautama of India but he rejected the worldly riches and abandoned the reigns of power when...
Religion/History/Biographies Pages 170

☐ **The Complete Works of Guy de Maupassant** by *Guy de Maupassant* ISBN: 1-59462-157-8 $16.95
"For days and days, nights and nights, I had dreamed of that first kiss which was to consecrate our engagement, and I knew not on what spot I should put my lips..."
Fiction/Classics Pages 240

☐ **The Art of Cross-Examination** by *Francis L. Wellman* ISBN: 1-59462-309-0 $26.95
Written by a renowned trial lawyer, Wellman imparts his experience and uses case studies to explain how to use psychology to extract desired information through questioning.
How-to/Science/Reference Pages 408

☐ **Answered or Unanswered?** by *Louisa Vaughan* ISBN: 1-59462-248-5 $10.95
Miracles of Faith in China
Religion Pages 112

☐ **The Edinburgh Lectures on Mental Science (1909)** by *Thomas* ISBN: 1-59462-008-3 $11.95
This book contains the substance of a course of lectures recently given by the writer in the Queen Street Hall, Edinburgh. Its purpose is to indicate the Natural Principles governing the relation between Mental Action and Material Conditions...
New Age/Psychology Pages 148

☐ **Ayesha** by *H. Rider Haggard* ISBN: 1-59462-301-5 $24.95
Verily and indeed it is the unexpected that happens! Probably if there was one person upon the earth from whom the Editor of this, and of a certain previous history, did not expect to hear again...
Classics Pages 380

☐ **Ayala's Angel** by *Anthony Trollope* ISBN: 1-59462-352-X $29.95
The two girls were both pretty, but Lucy who was twenty-one who supposed to be simple and comparatively unattractive, whereas Ayala was credited, as her Bombwhat romantic name might show, with poetic charm and a taste for romance. Ayala when her father died was nineteen...
Fiction Pages 484

☐ **The American Commonwealth** by *James Bryce* ISBN: 1-59462-286-8 $34.45
An interpretation of American democratic political theory. It examines political mechanics and society from the perspective of Scotsman James Bryce
Politics Pages 572

☐ **Stories of the Pilgrims** by *Margaret P. Pumphrey* ISBN: 1-59462-116-0 $17.95
This book explores pilgrims religious oppression in England as well as their escape to Holland and eventual crossing to America on the Mayflower, and their early days in New England...
History Pages 268

www.bookjungle.com *email: sales@bookjungle.com fax: 630-214-0564 mail: Book Jungle PO Box 2226 Champaign, IL 61825*

QTY

The Fasting Cure *by* **Sinclair Upton** — ISBN: *1-59462-222-1* **$13.95**
In the Cosmopolitan Magazine for May, 1910, and in the Contemporary Review (London) for April, 1910, I published an article dealing with my experiences in fasting. I have written a great many magazine articles, but never one which attracted so much attention... New Age/Self Help/Health Pages 164

Hebrew Astrology *by* **Sepharial** — ISBN: *1-59462-308-2* **$13.45**
In these days of advanced thinking it is a matter of common observation that we have left many of the old landmarks behind and that we are now pressing forward to greater heights and to a wider horizon than that which represented the mind-content of our progenitors... Astrology Pages 144

Thought Vibration or The Law of Attraction in the Thought World — ISBN: *1-59462-127-6* **$12.95**
by **William Walker Atkinson** — *Psychology/Religion Pages 144*

Optimism *by* **Helen Keller** — ISBN: *1-59462-108-X* **$15.95**
Helen Keller was blind, deaf, and mute since 19 months old, yet famously learned how to overcome these handicaps, communicate with the world, and spread her lectures promoting optimism. An inspiring read for everyone... Biographies/Inspirational Pages 84

Sara Crewe *by* **Frances Burnett** — ISBN: *1-59462-360-0* **$9.45**
In the first place, Miss Minchin lived in London. Her home was a large, dull, tall one, in a large, dull square, where all the houses were alike, and all the sparrows were alike, and where all the door-knockers made the same heavy sound... Childrens/Classic Pages 88

The Autobiography of Benjamin Franklin *by* **Benjamin Franklin** — ISBN: *1-59462-135-7* **$24.95**
The Autobiography of Benjamin Franklin has probably been more extensively read than any other American historical work, and no other book of its kind has had such ups and downs of fortune. Franklin lived for many years in England, where he was agent... Biographies/History Pages 332

Name	
Email	
Telephone	
Address	
City, State ZIP	

☐ Credit Card   ☐ Check / Money Order

Credit Card Number	
Expiration Date	
Signature	

Please Mail to: Book Jungle
PO Box 2226
Champaign, IL 61825
or Fax to: 630-214-0564

ORDERING INFORMATION

web: *www.bookjungle.com*
email: *sales@bookjungle.com*
fax: *630-214-0564*
mail: *Book Jungle PO Box 2226 Champaign, IL 61825*
or PayPal *to sales@bookjungle.com*

Please contact us for bulk discounts

DIRECT-ORDER TERMS

**20% Discount if You Order
Two or More Books**
Free Domestic Shipping!
Accepted: Master Card, Visa,
Discover, American Express

www.ingramcontent.com/pod-product-compliance
Lightning Source LLC
Chambersburg PA
CBHW081232170426
43198CB00017B/2730